STATE OF VERMONT
DEPARTMENT OF LIBRARIES
MIDSTATE LIBRARY SERVICE CENTER
578 PAINE TPKE N
BERLIN, VT 05602

MEDICINE SHOW

Also by Mary Calhoun

KATIE JOHN
DEPEND ON KATIE JOHN
HONESTLY, KATIE JOHN!
THE HOUSE OF THIRTY CATS
WHITE WITCH OF KYNANCE
IT'S GETTING BEAUTIFUL NOW
OWNSELF

MEDICINE SHOW

CONNING PEOPLE AND MAKING THEM LIKE IT

by Mary Calhoun

Harper & Row, Publishers
New York, Hagerstown, San Francisco, London

ACKNOWLEDGMENTS

I wish to give special thanks to Cliff Mann for inspiring this history of medicine shows by telling his tales of the life.

I am grateful for the wealth of information found in: *Four White Horses and a Brass Band*, by Violet McNeal, Doubleday & Company, Inc., 1947; *The Golden Age of Quackery*, by Stewart Holbrook, The Macmillan Company, 1959; *Medicine Show*, by Malcolm Webber, Caxton Printers, 1941; *The Saturday Evening Post* articles: "Med Show," Sept. 14, 1929, and "Alagazam: The Story of Pitchmen, High and Low," Oct. 19, 1929, by Dr. N. T. Oliver (Nevada Ned), as told to Wesley Stout. (The poem by James Whitcomb Riley was quoted by Oliver in the *Saturday Evening Post* article "Med Show.")

Texas Charlie's pitch tale for Kickapoo Indian Sagwa is found in the papers of the Townsend Walsh Collection, New York Library for the Performing Arts, Lincoln Center, n.d.

Permission has been granted for material quoted from: "Three O'Clock Train" in *American Vaudeville, Its Life and Times*, by Douglas Gilbert, Dover Publications, Inc., 1940. *The Americans: A Social History of the United States, 1587–1914*, by J. C. Furnas, G. P. Putnam's Sons, 1969. "Some Personal Experiences in Medicine Show Buncombe," by Charles S. Mundell, *Haldeman-Julius Monthly*, 1925. "Some Memories of a Medicine Show Performer," by Mae Noell, *Theatre Quarterly* (U.K.), May–July 1974.

MEDICINE SHOW: CONNING PEOPLE AND MAKING THEM LIKE IT
Copyright © 1976 by Mary H. Wilkins
All rights reserved. No part of this book may be used or reproduced in any manner whatsoever without written permission except in the case of brief quotations embodied in critical articles and reviews. Printed in the United States of America. For information address Harper & Row, Publishers, Inc., 10 East 53rd Street, New York, N.Y. 10022. Published simultaneously in Canada by Fitzhenry & Whiteside Limited, Toronto.
FIRST EDITION

Library of Congress Cataloging in Publication Data
Calhoun, Mary.
  Medicine show.

  Bibliography: p.
  Includes index.
  SUMMARY: Describes the medicine shows that not only sold cure-all medicines but also provided entertainment to small towns from mid-nineteenth century to mid-twentieth century.
  1. Medicine shows—United States—Juvenile literature. [1. Medicine shows] I. Title.
GV1803.C34   1976   791.1   75-25417
ISBN 0-06-020929-1
ISBN 0-06-020930-5 lib. bdg.

To Copper Christopher Calhoun,
mutual grandson of the author
and Cliff Mann

Contents

1	THE BALLYHOO	1
2	THE WARM-UP McDonald's Indian Medicine Show	4
3	THE SHOW History of Medicine Shows	22
4	THE PITCH How Did They Do It?	43
5	THE AILMENTS AND THE MEDICINE "Now I Bring You This Miraculous Cure!"	63
6	THE ENTERTAINMENT "They Loved Us in Greenville"	88
7	COUNTING UP THE RECEIPTS Why Did They Do It?	104
	AFTERWORD	114
	Bibliography	122
	Glossary	126
	Index	131
	Picture Credits	136

1
THE BALLYHOO

Razzle-dazzle! Fast music and flashy color that made the blood zing, out there in the cornfields. "Come on, folks, I'm going to give you the chance of a lifetime! I offer you this miraculous medicine that—"

Conning people—cheating them and making them like it—that was the skill of the medicine showman. Almost like a magician, he convinced people to buy his medicine—"the world's greatest cure-all!"—although it might be nothing but rainwater and Epsom salts. Yet people spent hard-earned quarters and dollars to buy that "cure-all" year after year. How did the medicine man do it? Why did he do it? And why did people love it?

For nearly a century, traveling medicine shows were a colorful part of American life, with their fast-talking salesmen, their wonderfully named remedies and their entertainers who attracted the crowds. From the 1850s until the 1940s, medicine-selling troupes moved from town to town, first in wagons, much later in trucks, all of the vehicles gaudily painted to catch the eye. The shows' territory was mainly rural America, their audiences the folks from the farms and villages. Not a circus, not a carnival, a medicine show was basically an entertainment put on for the purpose of selling

Show wagon in Pasadena, California, about 1900.

medicine. Usually admission was free, because the man who often called himself "doctor" knew he could sell his tonics and liniments to those country people he called "the yokels." His persuasive lecture about the medicine was his "pitch," and the medicine showman came to be known as a "pitch doctor."

The medicine show business flourished most widely in the 1880s and the 1890s. Two giants, the Kickapoo Indian Medicine Company and Hamlin's Wizard Oil Company, maintained their medicine factories in the East and sent out up to thirty troupes apiece to sell their products by entertaining small-town America. At the same time, hundreds of smaller independent shows toured the Deep South, the Midwest and the Far West. Medicine show business was Big Business.

Large or small, the medicine shows generally followed the same format. First came the ballyhoo, the come-on. The ballyhoo, or bally, might be as big as a noon parade, with the show's musicians giving a concert from a bandwagon, or it might be a gimmick for attracting attention: If you were walking down the street and saw a distinguished-looking man in a colorful Chinese mandarin robe tying a blindfold over the eyes of a beautiful girl in a Chinese gown, wouldn't you stop to see what happened next?

The actual medicine show began with music and laughter to warm up the crowd—musicians playing lively numbers, comedians telling jokes. Next came the featured entertainment—vaudeville acts, comedy skits or a play. Then, when the people in the audience were full of good cheer and enjoyment, the show doctor took the stage. He gave his health lecture, sold his tonics and salves, pills and liniments, and retired to count the receipts. Last, the whole troupe came on stage for the finale of the show, and then everyone went home happy, especially the pitch doctor.

The wares he sold have come to be called quack medicines, nostrums that did little or nothing to heal the sick. Before 1907, there was no legal control over the ingredients in a formula sold as medicine. Patent or proprietary medicine was the name given to any concoction a person wanted to mix up, whether in a factory or in a barrel behind the barn. Yet in 1906, the American people spent $80 million to buy patent medicines from stores, from mail-order houses and from medicine shows. If the products were worthless, how did the medicine showman manage to sell his share?

How did the pitch doctor persuade the sober old farmer to buy a bottle of "cure-all"? Because he did. That farmer bought the bottle, or the tow sack full of bottles, and walked away happy. What's more, he went back to the same medicine show the next year and stood right up and told how that medicine had helped him.

By the 1930s, the public's fascination with medicine shows had declined; the medicine show era was near its end. Yet even in those Depression days, when nearly everyone was poor, certain medicine showmen could go back every year and make new sales to the farmers.

How did the showmen do it? Why could they go back?

2
THE WARM-UP
McDonald's Indian Medicine Show

Doc McDonald's Indian Medicine Show was one outfit that could go back to its customers—nearly always. Cliff Mann traveled with his family's show every summer of his boyhood in the late 1920s and 1930s, touring the small towns in the hills of Oklahoma, east Texas and Arkansas. Cliff's memories give a picture of how a medicine show operated and what life was like with a "tramp" medicine show during the Depression.

It was a small show, numbering at most about a dozen men and women who doubled as musicians and actors. Cliff's uncle, Jude McDonald, was the pitch doctor and owner of the show. Cliff's father, Eugene Richard "Happy" Mann, was chief comedian and musician, and he specialized in "guitar picking." Doc McDonald's wife often acted and sang in the performances, but Cliff's mother "absolutely refused to have anything to do with the stage." She was raised a staunch Methodist with no experience at performing, Cliff said, and "she was too backward to get into the swing of things on the stage."

Since the 1880s, many traveling shows had featured Indians and Indian medicine, but the pitch doctor running the show usually was a white man. Jude McDonald toured as one of the few pitch doctors who actually was an Indian.

Cliff's family joined the show in 1928. His father had been a boot and harness maker, and he earned a good living at his work. But what Happy Mann really liked to do was to play the guitar and sing and clown at acting—he liked to perform. And there was no audience in a boot and saddle shop to watch a man make a boot. When his sister's husband came along with a medicine show that was doing a good business, Happy Mann was glad to join the troupe. Although his wife, Alice, didn't want to perform, she too liked the idea of a more adventurous life, traveling the road. So for the next ten years, it was *Move on, Hit the road!* for the Mann family.

Cliff was up on the stage right away. He was eight years old when the family started traveling with the show, and he played "little boy" roles in the plays presented by the troupe. Although the hired actors and musicians sometimes had children, Cliff was the only child who traveled and worked consistently with the show. That first year on the road Cliff's six-year-old sister died of pneumonia, and his youngest brother was born. Another brother, Joe, was about five years old at that time, too young to take part in the show. A pattern of life developed for the children: In the summers they traveled with the family; in the winters they were dropped off to live with their Irish grandmother on a farm in Oklahoma. There they attended the nearby Indian Agency grade school, where about half the schoolchildren were Indian.

Cliff said, "At first I wasn't wild about going out on the road in the summers. I'd just as soon stay on the farm with Grandma Sullivan. But after a while I was hooked, and you couldn't have gotten me out of show business."

At the age of fifty-five, Cliff Mann looked back and told about his medicine show years:

Medicine show coming! Boy, how the kids and dogs would run

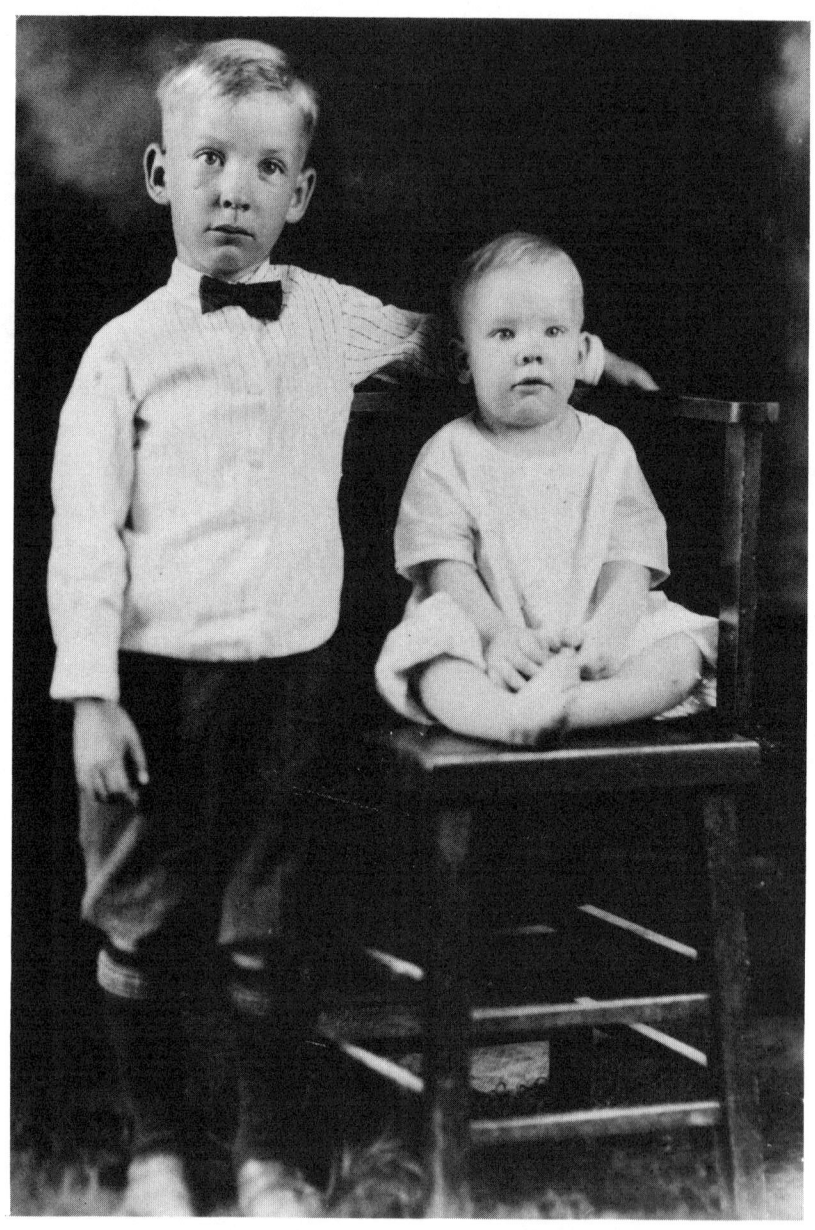
Cliff Mann, 8, and baby brother Joe.

out to see us! We'd come tearing down those dirt roads in a cloud of dust, driving big old white cars all painted up, rigged fancy with steer horns on the radiators. The farm women would run out, too; they knew now there'd be a little color in their lives for a few nights.

We were entertainment coming where they didn't see entertainment from one year to the next. Because we played in little towns where they didn't have a movie theater, a drugstore, a doctor—or a sheriff.

You see, they were con artists, my dad and my uncle, the way they ran their Indian medicine show. But they put on a good show, and that medicine worked—we took it ourselves. I'll tell you, all those good old farmers sure were glad to see our medicine show coming. I was proud of the show, proud to be show people.

My dad was one-quarter Cherokee Indian, but my uncle by marriage was the real Indian of the group. A Choctaw, he had long, coal-black hair, wore feathers for the image. He was a big man, real nice feller, but he could be impressive. Uncle Jude was a ham actor, just plain ham. During the day all he lived for was performing in the show that night. Up on that stage he was in a world of his own. Jude had a talent for selling, and I guess back in those Depression days there wasn't an awful lot to sell. So he sold medicine—tonic, Magic Corn Salve, liniment.

Doc really was an Indian medicine man, and his true Indian remedies were the cures that worked best. He knew herbs from the creek bottoms; he knew to go down in a wet cave and scrape off green mold to make a poultice to put on a boil. When we got boils or the itch, Doc would heal us up with his herbs and molds from nature. Yet he sold the standard medicine show items to the public. It was the hoked-up tonic and the Magic Corn Salve that those country people would lay out their dimes and their eggs for.

Our biggest seller was Uncle Jude's special tonic, which was called McDonald's Compound. We'd make it in a washtub and use rainwater, because rainwater has a kind of a peculiar taste anyway. And then we'd put in Epsom salts, cake coloring, a little Black-Draught with that—that's a purgative, of course—and some alcohol (old moonshine) to perk people up a little bit. But I'll guarantee you, if you took half a bottle of that tonic in the spring of the year, it would do just exactly what it said it would do: It would perk you up. You'd *better* get perky. It would clean you all the way.

Our other big item was Doc McDonald's Magic Corn Salve. Oxydol laundry soap. My folks would buy it in great big boxes, and they'd boil the Oxydol until it jelled, and let it cool in pie pans. Then they'd cut it in little chunks, and they'd wrap each one up in a paper with a label on it. Every night you soaked your feet in hot water, then you took this little bar of Magic Corn Salve and rubbed it on the corn on your toe, and you kept soaking your feet for five or ten minutes and rubbing this bar on the corn. . . . Well, ninety percent of the corns back then weren't corns, they were dirt calluses. So all they had to do was wash their feet! And the people loved it, because they wouldn't have washed their feet any other way.

Of course, to sell medicine you've got to attract the crowds. Doc and Happy were experts at come-ons and advertising. When we'd get to one of those little bitty towns, we'd put up signs that said Doc McDonald's Indian Medicine Show would be there all week. We'd tack up handbills on trees and around mailboxes by the road. Sometimes we'd stop at a church on Sunday and tell two or three women, and of course they'd spread the news. Those farm women worked hard, and they were glad to come to the show. But the best part of our ballyhoo was the little street attractions Dad and Uncle Jude would put on.

I remember one of the demonstrations my dad used to pull on

a street corner to show people how strong that corn salve was. He'd get old dress patterns that they used to give away at dry-goods stores; they were in about three or four colors, but it was cheap, cheap color. My dad would take this corn salve, and he'd wet it, and he'd run it over that picture. Then he'd take a handkerchief and a spoon, and he'd transfer the image onto the handkerchief. Proving how powerful that medicine was!

Of course, just water would have done it, because that dress-pattern ink was so cheap it would come off anyway.

First, though, you had to draw your street crowd. One time my dad picked the doggonedest argument with Uncle Jude in front of the general store. Doc hit Dad with a double paddle—a faked-up paddle with two boards hinged to make a pop when it's swung, as if a person had really been whammed with that paddle. It's used in comedy routines, and in fact, that's probably where we get the term "slapstick" comedy.—Well, when Doc hit Dad, the two boards made a loud smack, and Dad fell down and kicked his legs and groaned something awful.

One old lady watched all that, and she hollered for the town marshal. The marshal looked, and he says, "Why, I seen those two jokers here last year. They're not fighting, lady, they're just conning you." And he walked on.

Sometimes Doc and Dad would put on a little comedy skit; but whatever, once they had a crowd gathered, they'd pass out the handbills and tell everybody to come on out to the show that night. There was no charge for the sidewalk attractions, but they'd gig you once they got you into the show.

We'd set up in a field on the edge of town, where some farmer had given us permission. Sometimes we had a tent, sometimes we didn't. If there was a tent, we might charge a dime for admission; otherwise, there was no charge to watch. We'd get you later! We had a folding platform with canvas curtains for the actors to come from behind, and the people sat on little folding chairs or benches we carried along. We lit the show with lanterns, except when we were doing good. Then we had generators for lights, burned about five bulbs. Some of those people down in Arkansas I don't believe had ever seen an electric light.

But say, did those country people love the show! First the musicians would come out and warm everybody up, singing and playing guitar, fiddle, banjo, maybe a mandolin. My dad's specialty was, he was a guitar picker. He picked the strings with all his fingers, and that amazed a lot of people. Then Dad would do a buck-and-wing dance, which is a comic tap dance where you fling your legs around, and he'd wear those clown shoes with extra-long toes. He'd jump up, dancing, then slap those long toes on the platform, and they'd pop, and people would jump and laugh.

Next, a couple of the guys came out and did a comedy routine. We used to buy the comedy skit books from an outfit in Chicago. But the skits were just to bring everybody in and get them easy. When we'd get all those little suckers in there from all over the country, then we'd get down to business, the main attraction, The Play.

The play might be *Ten Nights in a Barroom* or *The Dying Cowboy*, but the one I remember best was *The Trail of the Lonesome Pine*, because I was in it. I played the pretty little blond boy, and I got killed every night, and then I was through. I was supposed to be playing on a steam engine, and it fell off a railroad trestle. We didn't have much in the way of props, so somebody behind the stage would knock over some boxes and cans, and then when the curtain opened again, I'd be lying there with a few boards on me. Of course they were talking about this all the time; there was one person who had to tell what all went on. The actors didn't speak many lines; mostly they pantomimed the action and sang. Then the whole troupe would have the big deal where they took me up through the pines to bury me—for scenery we had a piece of canvas painted with a pine tree—and they'd sing "Trail of the Lonesome Pine."

But understand, they didn't show the play all the way through without interruption. Right about the time when the play really got interesting, they shut it off, and then's when the pitch took place!

That's when Doc McDonald came out and sold his medicine. And he was the man the crowd had been waiting for, because he never showed himself until then. He'd come out in a white jacket, with his hair really long and black, feathers on his head, a big man up there on the stage—impressive.

Jude talked long and high-pressure, gradually building it up how wonderful his medicine was. Indians knew the secrets of nature, he'd say, and he was about to share his knowledge, his gift of health, with these people.

Doc would say, "There was this old lady on her deathbed, dying of dyspepsia, and she took my nature-brewed tonic, and she was up eating fried sweet potato the very next day!"

Then it was, "You there! I can see you're wanting this good tonic. You got a dime? No? Well, you take this bottle of McDonald's Compound and bring me back a half dozen eggs tomorrow." Or, "I'll swap you all this medicine for a tow sack of potatoes."

And they'd do it. They'd be back there the next day with the goods.

At the time of the pitch, that's when they started selling the candy, too. That's when we had our big diamond-ring contest. You see, every night they sold candy, and it was a popularity contest. Whoever bought the most candy boxes during the show and turned in the box tops at the end of the week with a girl's name on them, she got the diamond ring, free. And it was a real diamond, but I guarantee you, you had to look awful close to see that little feller. That candy—if you had dentures or bad teeth! It was saltwater taffy, and it was ten years old. It was so hard you couldn't chew it; you had to suck it.

But we never did anything that hurt people. Our medicine couldn't hurt you, because if you took too much tonic, you'd just go a little faster. We took the tonic ourselves, maybe watered it down a little. People got their money's worth when they bought our medicine. We never had anything to do with those real con artists, the carnies, who took your money and didn't give you a blamed thing for it. Them and their shell games that you could never win! Of course you couldn't win your bet on which walnut shell the pea was under, because while the carnie was shifting those shells around, he'd palmed the pea. We *never* played where the carnivals were set up, wouldn't go near them. We looked down on those people. They weren't show people. *We* were show people. We were entertainers!

After the show at night, it was a big thing to play music for dances. Those country people couldn't get enough of our music. They'd say, "Come on out to the schoolhouse—or the farmhouse—and play us a square dance. We've got food, moonshine." We'd eat potatoes, beans, fried chicken, and they'd put pallets down on the floor in another room for us kids, and then, boy, would they dance! Dad and the other musicians would play guitar and scrape fiddle all night. And when the folks got tired of dancing, my dad would strum his guitar and sing for them. He must have known a thousand songs, but he loved to sing the blues the best, songs like "The Jailhouse Blues."

I never learned to play the guitar or sing like my dad, but I did plenty of work with the show. Besides acting in the plays, I ran around selling, when Doc finished his sales pitch. I delivered the medicine from the stage out into the crowd, and I sold the candy boxes. Other times I helped the women mix up the medicine and put the Doc McDonald labels on the tonic and corn salve. And of course, I helped load and unload the equipment every time we moved.

By the time I was twelve I got twenty-five cents a week as my salary. I'd buy a big sack of Golden Grain tobacco for a nickel—we all learned to smoke when we were young, because I suppose that was the only vice we could get away with—and I'd buy four books at the drugstore when we'd get to a bigger town. They were old books that hadn't sold, so their covers had been torn off, and I could get them for a nickel apiece. I'd buy the books about World War I Flying Aces and the Charlie Chan detective stories and the cowboy westerns. I had to have books, had to have something to read.

Cliff told how a medicine show traveled in the 1930s and what everyday life was like for a boy with a tramp show.

Come the end of the week, then we'd move on. I mean, our way of life was on the road. Uncle Jude generally had an old bus all painted up with Indian signs and his name on it and curtains at the windows, and that's where we carried the show equipment. Sometimes we had a flatbed truck to carry the tent, when we had a tent. But the rest of us always traveled in old house-cars that we built. We'd take an automobile, strip the body off, just leave the front seat, and we'd build a little house on it. Inside there was room for one bed and a homemade wood-burning stove to cook on. When my mother tried to bake biscuits, we'd go down the road with smoke just a-coming out the stovepipe sticking out of the car.

We bought big old cars for about fifty dollars apiece: Essex, Hupmobile, Willis Knight, Page, Durant, Packard; but my favorite was a Dodge, the old Dodge Fast-Four. That was the best to build a house-car onto. You'd try to buy a popular car, so you could get parts and tires along the way. Fifty dollars didn't buy you much of a car. Those old cars would wear out about every six months, and then you'd go buy another one for fifty dollars.

Traveling with the show, I learned to drive as soon as I could reach the pedals. And I got pretty good at it, except that I ran over my dad once. He was in front, cranking the car, and I was at the steering wheel, both of us trying to get the blamed thing started. I forgot it was in gear, so the car came off the prop-up in back and jumped forward. It didn't hurt him, but it sure made him mad. My dad was "Happy" onstage, but oh my, he was terrible to get along with after the show. He had quite a temper, and I guess I was good at provoking him. Over the years we had many an argument.

But talk about car trouble—continually! Perpetual car trouble! Everything you did yourself, overhaul the motors, the transmission, because there were no repair garages in those little towns where we traveled. For heavy work sometimes we'd take the car to a blacksmith shop. But back then everybody carried two trunks if they could, huge square trunks. Used to eat off of them, and they made real good props to stick under your car when you jacked up the front end to work on the transmission. And flats! We'd patch the inner tubes with those old rubberized patches that you glued on, and we'd pump up the tires by hand. Those days, if you broke down, nobody would pass you up. You didn't drive by anybody in trouble. Except for flats. Flats were so common nobody stopped for flats. *Everybody* had flats!

Of course, those roads we drove tore up the tires. It was only around the cities that we'd come on concrete. The roads we drove were ten percent gravel and ninety percent dirt. Sand was the worst, because the sand would tear up the transmission, or we'd get stuck in it. We tried to stay away from those rock roads, too, loose granite rocks that would tear up the tires. Most of our circuit for the show, my folks pretty well knew the roads, and they stayed on dirt roads wherever they could, because they were the best of the pick.

Traveling from town to town, we camped along the way, and we had us some good times around the campfire, singing of an evening and clapping our hands to the music. Dad was quite an educated feller, so he'd read the Bible to us, quote Scripture and preach to us. My Uncle Jude, he was the storyteller. He'd tell us outlaw stories about Jesse James and the Dalton boys, said he personally knew 'em—he might have. Sometimes when there were enough of us kids, we made up games to play at night, ideas we got from Tom Sawyer and Huckleberry Finn stories. We had to have imagination, I guess, to be in show business.

The closest we ever came to a tourist court was once in a while when we'd pull in at one of the old wagon yards. A wagon yard looked like a fort, because it had a high board fence around it and a big wooden door that was closed and barred at night. For twenty-five cents you could drive in, and they had stalls all around the edge of it. The stalls had awnings; you could pull your house-car or your wagon under the awnings, and each stall had fresh hay, if you needed it for your horse. Then in the center of the wagon yard there was a covered area with big cast-iron pots, where the women could do their wash. The men would sit around and visit, and all of us kids there for a night would get acquainted and play.

But camping by a creek was a way of life for us. We washed in the creek, and we ate out of it. First we'd all wash ourselves and wash up the show—the canvases on the folding seats, you had to keep those clean. Then we'd grapple the fish, run our hands along under the creek banks and catch catfish, and we'd fry up the fish. My mother and the other women would gather pokes of greens from along the creek banks and cook up the greens to go with the catfish. Or we had our bullfrog eats and our crawdad eats. We'd get out on a creek together, and we'd all gig frogs, cook the frog legs and crawdad tails. But sometimes the creeks would dry up, no fish, no green stuff. . . .

My mother was the world's worst cook, because she never had anything to cook.

You see, there was no money in the medicine show business in those Depression days. Oh, we did all right until about 1931, but then more and more people were out of work, and they didn't have cash to spend on tonic and corn salve. So we just survived. If we could make enough money to buy gasoline and flour, sugar and coffee, that was about it. As a kid I was always hungry. It became a way of life to be hungry. You got used to it, and after a while you didn't notice so much. To keep from being hungry I would pick up a little piece of tar off the railroad tracks, just to have something to chew on.

My favorite food, if I could get it, was hot biscuits and country butter—oh boy! And even better, biscuits with cream gravy and bacon. Pork and beans in a can—we seldom got that. If we had a really good week with the show, we'd all go to a café and eat chili—ten cents a bowl, with crackers and ketchup, lots of ketchup.

Besides food, all of us show kids had one ambition: clothes. That's why I hate overalls to this day, because I never had anything but overalls to wear when I was a boy.

Back then a gold watch and a gun were your bank account. Of course, you'd use your gun to shoot rabbit and squirrel for food, if you had ammunition. But if you'd get into a sickness spell, get into a bind and need some money for a road stake, you'd trade off that gun. Or your watch. My folks never had much of anything, because they always traded things off when we needed money.

My dad could have stayed put and made a real living. He was a boot maker, one of the best. There were always boot com-

Happy Mann with guitar, about 1930; chief musician and comedian with Doc McDonald's Indian Medicine Show.

panies wanting him to work for them. At times I wished he'd do that, earn us a real living, so I'd have enough to eat and decent clothes to wear. But you couldn't chain Dad in one place. My mother was the same way. It was always *Move on, Hit the road!*

So it was a lonely life. Kids in towns where we'd stop, they'd say, "Where you from?" Well, we weren't *from* noplace; we weren't going *to* noplace; and we couldn't stay where we were. In those days there wasn't any back, any future. You just went from day to day.

It was really humiliating when we'd get to bigger towns to stock up on medicine supplies. In the little towns we show people were quite the *thing*. But in the big towns the kids would call me "blanket-ass." Because they'd see Uncle Jude and Dad dressed up like Indians, you know. It rubbed, after I got old enough to know different. The way to handle it was . . . rough. I used to think if I had two good fists and something to eat I could win the war. So I'd fight.

Sometimes, though, the adults tormented us show kids. They'd grab us by the ears and run us away from their kids. Then there wasn't anything I could do about that, just back off. People in the bigger towns resented travelers, didn't want us coming in. During the Depression they didn't have enough jobs for their own.

But my family, we knew you couldn't ever give up. People would die; we'd wrap them in a blanket, get permission to bury and drive on, maybe come back, maybe not. And we didn't forget those people. But life was on the road, and it could be good around the next bend, down in the next town. In that next little town those folks were sure gonna be glad to see our medicine show coming.

Your friends were on the road. Every creek bottom, every campground, there was always somebody there beside you. People all camping together, telling their stories—they were your friends. You didn't try to sell medicine to those people; you gave it to them. At a campground, if we had flour and the folks next to us didn't have any for their hoecakes (that's kind of a sick hotcake), Mother would split her flour with them. The same, they'd split their lard with her.

They were the willow-furniture makers, the barn-sign painters, the tinkers and scissors grinders, who followed their regular routes. We show kids stuck pretty close with the willow-furniture kids, and it was a tramp sign painter who got me interested in painting pictures. Willow furniture is like wicker, woven out of green willow—chairs, two-place settees, hanging porch swings. The willow makers didn't stay around long after they sold their furniture, because when that green willow dried out, it didn't look so good. It came loose, because it was only put together with shingle nails. The barn painters were ones the farmers looked forward to, though, because it was the only time they got that kind of service. A farmer could get his barn painted free, if the sign painter could letter in on the side of the barn a big advertisement for his company's medicine, work clothes, beer or whatever.

The campers might be the chalk people, who sold chalk dogs, dolls and lawn ornaments. They'd form those things in molds they made, then paint them up. Or they might be the crepe-paper-flower makers, and sometimes they'd sell a whole bunch of crepe-paper flowers dipped in wax for arbors for church camp meetings. They were all of them traveling, selling anything they could, doing anything they could to survive in those hard times.

I got so I knew everybody on the road in the Southwest, knew where they'd be. That kind of life, you didn't have to take a college course to learn psychology. You learned *people.* You learned how to get with a man—farmer, logger, outlaw, whoever.

Every once in a while we'd run into another medicine show traveling the same territory. Maybe it was run by a Cherokee Indian doctor, maybe a show with a magician, maybe a feller selling something called Black Diamond Snake Oil. We all had our code. If another show came into a town where you were playing, they'd stop and camp and visit with you, go to your show, maybe even help you. But they'd cover up the signs on their cars, never interfere or set up to rival you. We'd all swap information on which towns were good to sell, which towns were hard to sell, which towns had tough policemen.

Because, you see, any medicine show could get run out of town. We tried to keep our show clean, to stay on the right side of people. We didn't even have sleight-of-hand card tricks, because some of those folks thought cards were sinful. Yet it was real simple to shut down a show in those days. If you made the mistake of trying to sell medicine in a town where there was a drugstore, and the druggist didn't like your competition, he would just tell the marshal to run you out of town. No legal procedure—and certainly no government inspection of our medicine back then. The marshal would just come around and say, "You better hit the trail." No argument. We left.

Now the Indian medicine man, Uncle Jude, they got after him a few times because of religion. They figured maybe he was a witch. One time we got way down South, and there were some Baptists who called him an atheist, a heathen. Besides, they had gotten drunk on Doc's tonic, and that made them mad, too. Can't say as I blame them. So they got up a crew to come after Doc McDonald. Well, we had learned not to spread ourselves out too thin in that country, so we moved fast. You wouldn't believe how far and how fast you could travel on a flat tire!

My family, though, they could always go back—most places. Doc McDonald's Indian Medicine Show had a regular circuit, and we'd go back year after year. My folks were pretty smart; they didn't make too many enemies. People would get up and testify how good the corn salve had worked on them, how the tonic had cured their backaches and ulcers. Shoot, all that was the matter with those farmers was calluses and constipation. We did them a service, brought them good laxatives and entertainment to boot!

Proud? Yeah, I was proud of our show. We were pioneers in show business. But pride, it might have been a necessity. Back in those days it kinda got mixed up whether it was pride or a necessity. It wasn't all just the show business; it was the other thing you kept thinking about—the way of life, bumming around during the Depression. It was a way of life that's gone, and I hope to heck it stays gone for kids today. I realize now I was never a *kid*, and I miss that. And yet, now I'm out of show business, I miss it, too. If there was any money in it, that's not a bad way to live, selling something while you're entertaining people.

3
THE SHOW
History of Medicine Shows

Selling medicine by offering entertainment . . . Cliff Mann's family, with its Indian medicine show, was following a practice that had gone on for a hundred years in the United States and for centuries before that in Europe. Sometimes the amateur "doctor" presented a large troupe of entertainers; sometimes he himself was the sole performer. But generally through the years he found medicine a good item to sell. Especially wonder medicine. Because nearly everyone gets sick at some time and needs healing, and many a person in pain hopes for a sure cure for his ailment. The glamorous act—the razzle-dazzle—of a medicine showman in the streets could convince people that here at last was a Healer who knew the secrets of sickness and health.

Consider the aura of self-importance the High German Doctor created in order to sell his medicines at a London fair in the mid-1700s. In his novel *The World Went Very Well Then,* Walter Besant told how the stage was set for the dramatic appearance of the medicine man. At first, clowns prance on the outdoor platform, walk a tightrope and joke with the passersby. Suddenly a man dressed in yellow and black blows a tin trumpet and calls "Room for the doctor!" Mounted on a black horse, the High German Doctor slowly rides toward the stage. He is dressed in a long gown of black velvet, and on his head is the crimson velvet cap that signifies a university doctor. Attached to the saddle is a kind of lectern holding a thick book, which the learned man reads as he rides, as if not to lose one moment of study.

A placard on the stage declares that the doctor has been physician to the Sophy (ruler) of Persia and to the Great Mogul, tooth drawer to the King of Morocco and corn cutter to the Emperor of Trebizonde, the Grand Turk and Prester John.

What is he selling? "The Cataplasma Diabolicum or Vulnerary Decoction of Monkshood, which heals wounds in twenty-four hours. If taken with the Electuary Pacific—show the Electuary, varlets!—it heals in a couple of hours." Who wouldn't buy?

Through the centuries, a European medicine show consisted simply of a "doctor" selling his wares on city streets with the assistance of two or three hired musicians, clowns or acrobats. The *traveling* medicine show developed in America in the nineteenth century. With all that wide-open frontier country of rubes spread out before him, the medicine man took his show on the road. By the end of the century the settled areas of the nation and its frontiers had been crisscrossed by medicine men offering full evenings of drama, comedy and dance, Indian shows, minstrel shows, parades and bands playing on gold-plated instruments.

In 1800 the American Revolutionary War had been over for seventeen years. The thirteen colonies had become the United States of America and grown to seventeen states with the admission of Ohio in 1803. There were no paved roads between the small towns and villages, and settled people seldom traveled more than a few miles from home in their wagons or on horseback. In the 1820s, the region around the Great Lakes and along the Mississippi River was the frontier—forests, swamps and unplowed prairies. There the trappers hunted fur-bearing animals and traded with the Indians, gradually leading the way westward for the pioneering farmers, ranchers and miners who followed. Until 1880, those pioneers could find large areas of unsettled frontier land in America, often free for the taking. The frontier of the U.S. was not declared closed by the Superintendent of Census until 1890, when at last there were more than two persons per square mile in most areas. There was no longer a definite frontier line of unsettled land.

In the early 1800s, medical care was very limited compared to present-day standards. Trained doctors were few—in 1775, only 400 of them held university medical degrees. Until 1765, when the first medical school was opened in Philadelphia, men had to travel by ship to Europe to study at medical centers, or else apprentice under an established doctor for four to seven years. Hospitals were found only in cities, and only in the larger towns were there apothecary shops that sold the known medicines of the time. In the less populated areas, pioneer physicians on horseback carried in their saddlebags a pharmacy of quinine and calomel, salts and aloes, sassafras and bergamot, ingredients they would mix up in the patients' kitchens as needed for certain illnesses. Still earlier, during colonial times, it was the Yankee peddler, traveling the muddy or rocky roads from town to settlement, who brought most people their medicines. Along with his needles, thread and tinware, the peddler sold cubeb, anise, cascara, cinchona and gentian to the farm wives, who used those in home brews to combat their families' ails.

Few doctors knew what caused most illnesses, for there was little scientific knowledge of internal medicine to instruct them. The idea that germs caused disease was unknown—the germ theory of disease was not proved until the late 1800s. People suffered and died from yellow fever and malaria, and no one, not even the doctors, knew that those plagues were caused by disease-bearing mosquitoes. Vaccination against smallpox had only been introduced in the 1700s, and the practice was still mistrusted and feared by many. For the treatment of tubercular patients, a prominent Philadelphia doctor, Benjamin Rush, prescribed horseback riding, because it was believed that the smell of horses was good for weak lungs. No one knew what cancer was or how to treat it.

And so the quack doctor offered wonder medicines to cure all ailments.

Since colonial times, patent medicines had been offered for sale by individuals, although few of the concoctions were actually registered with the U.S. Patent Office. "Patent" medicines were proprietary medicines that could be any mixture of herbs, spices or snake oil a person decided to manufacture as a curative. A proprietor of a remedy might sincerely believe it would cure, or he might simply be after an easy dollar. It didn't matter legally, because there were no governmental controls on the ingredients that went into a curative or the claims the proprietor made about the medicine's ability to cure.

In 1692, the *Boston Almanac* published an advertisement for Aqua anti torminales, "which if timely taken, it not only cures the Griping of the Guts and the Wind Cholick, but preventeth that woeful Distemper of the Dry Belly Ach. Sold by Benj Harris at the London-Coffee House in Boston." In 1711 a concoction called Tuscarora Rice was advertised as a cure for consumption (tuberculosis). As the use of the printing press grew, so did the advertisement of patent medicines in newspapers, almanacs and circulars. By the nineteenth century the sale of patent medicines had become a thriving business and a main source of advertising revenue for smaller newspapers.

Some medicine makers were content to sell their wares from shops in towns; but others with a flair for showmanship took their medicine out on the roads to the people. In the rural areas they saw the perfect combination of people's needs: a lack of adequate medicine combined with a lack of entertainment.

In the early part of the nineteenth century, the medicine man himself was the whole show. His forerunner, the Yankee peddler, might blow a tune on his tin horn to announce his approach to a farm, and in his wagon he might carry a fox in a cage or a trained dog that did a few tricks. But the true medicine showman provided more razzmatazz. One of those was Professor Popple, who claimed to know the "Secret Arts and Herbal Virtues of the Great Indian Chiefs of the Seneca and Cayuga tribes." To sell his Elixir of Life, which could be used internally or externally, he performed as a fire-eater and put on a magic show. In the 1820s he changed his name to Old Doc Hashalew, advertised his medicine in Central New York weekly newspapers and tramped the towpaths of the Erie Canal. Every night by torchlight he lectured on his magical medicine and ate fire to amaze his customers.

In the following years, traveling medicine men added to the entertainment: a banjo player, a comic dancer, a comedy skit, a play put on by a company of actors.

By far the most popular melodrama in the 1850s was *Uncle Tom's Cabin*, and any showman bringing the play to a Northern town was guaranteed an audience. Based on the best-selling anti-slavery novel by Harriet Beecher Stowe, the play featured the beloved black man, Uncle Tom; Eliza, who fled over the ice of the Ohio River toward freedom in the North; and the wicked slave overseer, Simon Legree. The emotion-tugging play and novel aroused such feeling in the North for the abolition of slavery that President Abraham Lincoln believed *Uncle Tom's Cabin* helped cause the Civil War. By 1860, theatrical troupes and medicine men were taking as many as twenty *Tom* or *Tommer* shows on circuits of the small towns in the North and the West along the upper Mississippi River. Of course, the smart showman didn't take the play into the South, where the white audiences might have taken offense at the portrayal of Southerners.

After the Civil War, a type of medicine show with more universal appeal, both in the North and in the South, began to develop —the Indian medicine show.

Poster advertising Uncle Tom's Cabin, *a play often presented by medicine shows.*

When Cliff Mann's uncle, Jude McDonald, came along in the 1930s, he told the farmers: "I am bringing you the gift of health in my nature-brewed tonic." The Indian—strong, pure, wise in herbs—surely the Indian knew the secrets of nature and could heal every ailment, people reasoned. The first French explorers and woodsmen had depended on Indian treatment of wounds and sores with poultices of herbs. Many a settler had been treated with remedies by the "yarb and root doctor," who gathered his herbs and roots from forest and field. A kind of mystical belief grew up about the red man's powers as a natural physician.

An early Indian-medicine book for home use was *The Indian Doctor's Dispensatory*, by Peter Smith, published in Cincinnati in 1813. To capitalize on people's trust in Indian medicines, other books followed, among them *The Indian Doctor's Receipt Book*, *The Indian Guide to Health* and *The North American Indian Doctor, or Nature's Method of Curing and Preventing Disease According to the Indians*.

Patent medicines began to pose as Indian tonics—"Nature's Gift to Nature's Children," as one advertisement phrased it. White men like Professor Popple posed as Indian doctors as they traveled in their two-horse buggies from settlement to homestead on the frontiers.

It was John E. Healy, however, who used the Indian medicine pitch to develop medicine shows into Big Business. In the 1880s and 1890s his Kickapoo Indian Medicine Company sent numerous troupes touring the East and the Midwest; his medicine factory at New Haven, Connecticut, turned out bottles of Indian Sagwa by the millions; and the "Kicks" shows became legendary in the medicine show business.

Actually, the wits of three men put the Kickapoo Indian Medicine Company together. Healy had the idea, Texas Charlie Bigelow worked out the pitch and Nevada Ned Oliver developed the show.

When the three men sat down in a hotel room in Philadelphia

in 1881 to plan their Indian show, each came with solid experience at pitching medicine. Healy had entered the business with a liniment he'd mixed up and called King of Pain. His first big troupe for selling this painkiller was Healy's Hibernian Minstrels, the performers rigged in Irish costume and jigging on the stage to Irish ballads. Next he teamed with Dr. E. H. Flagg, successful merchant of liver pads and of a Pain Balm that later was to become Kickapoo Indian Oil. To sell the liver pads and Pain Balm, Healy and Flagg organized several traveling units, each with three entertainers and a "doctor." Texas Charlie was hired on as a doctor and Nevada Ned as a banjo player, thus getting their first experience at working with Healy.

Charles Bigelow had been a Bee County, Texas, farmboy until a medicine showman came along and dazzled him. After Doctor Yellowstone breezed through selling his Herbs of Life, Charles foresook the plow, let his hair grow down past his shoulders, learned a set of magic tricks, acquired a four-horse coach and became Texas Charlie, "versed in the lore of the Indian medicine man."

Nevada Ned Oliver was reared in Philadelphia by a Baptist pastor, and was studying for the ministry himself when he dropped his studies at Yale University to go on the stage. Before long he was apprenticing in the medicine show business, playing the banjo and peddling painkiller for Healy. Ned worked for several showmen, then toured the South independently to sell polishing irons—irons with heels rounded to polish a "boiled" shirt to a high gloss. With money in his pocket, Nevada Ned Oliver rejoined Healy and Bigelow to give birth to the most famous Indian show of them all.

At first Healy envisioned a store in which a few hired Indians would sit around a steaming cauldron of medicine inside a teepee. The medicine would be the Indians' ancient formula of roots, herbs and bark that Cured All, ladled out to people who would bring their own containers.

Texas Charlie objected that "nobody wants to carry home medi-

Texas Charlie (Charles Bigelow) advertising Kickapoo Indian Sagwa and featured on a medicine show program.

PICTURESQUE
INDIAN VILLAGE!

ON CIRCUS LOT,

Cor. HUDSON AVE. and SWAN ST.,

Every Night at 8 O'Clock, and Wednesday and Saturday Afternoons at 2:30 O'Clock.

PROGRAMME.

1. A Sight of a Life-Time.

A group of Indian Men and Women in their native Songs and Dances, with an interesting Lecture on their ways, customs and habits, by

TEXAS CHARLIE.

2. Classic Groupings.

LEVANION, LEXINGTON AND JOHNSON.

3. MARINE CABLE WIRE,

MR. GEORGE LA ROSE.

4. INDIAN MEDICINE CEREMONY

Introducing the Horse and Buffalo Dance.

5. Fancy Rifle Shooting,

Holding the Rifle in twenty different positions, by the noted Scout and Indian Fighter, TEXAS CHARLIE. The Rifle used is from the celebrated Wesson Rifle Co., of Worcester, Mass.

6. Contortion Act,

By the celebrated Indian Artist, GUS JOHNSON.

7. EMPRESS OF THE AIR,

MISS MAUD OSWALD, on the Flying Rings. Ladies and Children need have no fear for Miss Oswald's safety, as she is quite at home in the air.

8. Indian Marriage Ceremony.

9. Exercises on the Horizontal Bar,

LA ROSE BROS., LEVANION AND LEXINGTON.
CLOWN LEVANION.

The World's Greatest Canine Instructor, the original and only

10 Prof. HARRY M. PARKER,

And his Wonderful New Mastodon Dog Circus. The best trained Dogs on earth. 10 Large Handsome Dogs 10. Introducing large English Greyhounds, Setters, Spaniels, Tans, French, Russian, and Italian Poodles. 2 GREAT CLOWN DOGS. The Funniest Animals on Earth, who will keep the audience in a roar of laughter from beginning to the finish of the act. 8 Wonderful Leaping Dogs 8. Including the Great Royal English Greyhounds FLY, HANLON, and NELGIER who leap a distance of 30 feet and a height of 15 feet. A truly wonderful performance.

Introducing his wonderful leaping cat SPOT, springing 15 feet high through a hoop of fire.

cine in a bucket." Instead, he suggested, "We'll say the Indians send us the medicine, and we bottle it for them." "Right!" said Nevada Ned. "We'll act as Indian Agents."

Sagwa was the name chosen for the tonic, and Texas Charlie worked out a pitch-tale about Sagwa's discovery. One version, published in circulars by Healy & Bigelow in the late 1880s, told it this way:

Sagwa's Surprising Story: How Texas Charlie's Life Was Saved By the Indians.

Some years ago Mr. Chas. Bigelow, now one of the proprietors of the famous Kickapoo Indian Remedies, was acting as a government scout in the Indian territory. He was known at that time as "Texas Charlie," and while on one of his expeditions was taken sick with a severe fever, and for a few days lay at death's door. During his sickness he was cared for by the Indian Chief and his family, in whose lodge he lay, so weak he could hardly raise his eyelids. An Indian doctor visited him, and gave him that now most famous of Indian remedies, Indian Sagwa, and by its use he was snatched from the jaws of death and restored to health, owing his life to the wonderful efficacy and curative power of this medicine. He then endeavored to persuade the Indians to give him the secret of its ingredients. This at first they refused to do, but after much persuasion and many discussions they at last partially yielded to his request, and the Chief of the Tribe sent East with Mr. Bigelow five of his most renowned medicine men, together with an ample supply of the roots, herbs, barks, gums, etc., used in the manufacture of their medicines. What started thus in a small way has ever since increased, and today there is manufactured from similar materials gathered by the Indians themselves, their famous remedies, which have done so much to alleviate suffering of every description.

Indians were hired, but none came from the little Kickapoo tribe. Healy seems to have picked the name "Kickapoo" simply because the name amused him. The first red men with the show were Iroquois—Chief Thunder Cloud and seven of his braves—and for several years the Iroquois tribe contributed most of the "Kickapoo"

Indians to the shows. Later, performers were drawn from the tribes of the Pawnee, Cree, Sioux and Cherokee, amongst others. The Kickapoo Medicine Company sometimes dealt through federal Indian agents, offering their Indian wards thirty dollars a month and room and board. The Indians—men, women, children, plus their mustangs—came to live at the "Principal Wigwam" in New Haven, and legend has it they numbered as many as three hundred.

In the first show, Chief Thunder Cloud and his braves did not perform—they simply provided atmosphere. Soon, however, Nevada Ned had the Indians doing war dances, pounding tom-toms, giving testimonials in their own language—which he "interpreted" —and staging panoramic raids on wagon trains. By that time, probably 1882, the Kickapoo Indian Village had made it to New York City's Broadway, tents pitched in the old Aquarium for the entire winter season. Nevada Ned had expanded his talents, too: After considerable practice as a marksman, he added his sharpshooting act to the Indian spectacular on Broadway. Showmen had exhibited Indians in New York before, but Indians in a medicine show were a novelty. People flocked to see the Kickapoo Camp and buy the Indian Sagwa, and the Kickapoo Indian Medicine Company grew with success. Some shows were large and played in one city for an entire season. Others were smaller traveling units, with as many as seventy-five units on the road at one point in the 1880s.

Ned Oliver, as "Indian Agent," managed a typical unit of twelve —six Indians and six other performers—that traveled from town to town, pitching tents in empty lots. On stage the Indians would sit in a half circle around Oliver, who, in Western scout costume, introduced each Indian. One Indian would then make an impassioned speech in his native language, which Oliver interpreted as a glowing tale of the marvelous properties of their medicines. At the end of his sales pitch three of the entertainers would break into fast music, three Indians would shout war whoops and beat their tom-toms and the other six would circulate through the crowd to sell

Indian Sagwa for one dollar a bottle, oil, vermifuge and salve for a quarter apiece. In each town Oliver would then place the medicines in drugstores to be sold on consignment for the Kickapoo Company.

Several stationary units were developed by Nevada Ned into full-fledged Wild West shows. A typical one played for a season in 1886 in the baseball park at Bergen Heights, New Jersey. A cast of seventy persons and twenty-eight horses took part in the events: a wagon train of pioneers pitching camp for the night, an Indian raiding party sneaking up, an attempted massacre, much shooting and screaming, then the cowboys riding in to the rescue. With broncobusting and trick shooting acts included, Oliver claimed to sell $3000 to $4000 worth of medicine a week at Bergen Heights.

At first, Nevada Ned was a third equal partner with Healy and Bigelow, but "I persuaded myself that I was too smart to need partners," he said in his reminiscenses in a 1929 *Saturday Evening Post* article. He left the Kickapoo Indian Medicine Company to form his own medicine show and at one time toured with a rival Chippewa Indian Medicine Company, which folded after a season. For many years, Oliver continued to work as pitch doctor for major medicine shows.

The Indian medicine show proved so popular that other showmen adopted the format. The most famous of the independent Indian medicine pitchmen of that time, Jim Lighthall, became known as the King of the Medicine Men. Long-haired, handsome, flashing diamonds on his western buckskins, Doc Lighthall seemed to mesmerize people into buying his Herbs of Joy. He put on the usual Indian show, complete with war whoops and display of Indian curios; but most of all, Jim Lighthall had charisma.

Hamlin's Wizard Oil Company was the other titan of medicine show business in the latter part of the nineteenth century. Compared to the razzle-dazzle of the Indian shows, the Hamlin image was all dignity, featuring refined music and a distinguished doctor. The medicine was sold from wagons drawn from town to town by

HAMLIN'S
WIZARD OIL

THE GREAT MEDICAL WONDER.

There is no Sore it will Not Heal, No Pain it will not Subdue.

HAMLIN'S COUGH BALSAM

PLEASANT TO TAKE
MAGICAL IN ITS EFFECTS.

HAMLIN'S
BLOOD AND LIVER PILLS
For Liver Complaint, Constipation,
AND ALL
Disorders of the Stomach and Digestive Organs.

PREPARED AT THE LABORATORY OF
HAMLINS WIZARD OIL COMPANY, CHICAGO, ILL.

handsome four- or six-horse teams. In each unit was a driver, a lecturer and a vocal-instrumental quartet, with a parlor organ built onto each wagon. The men always dressed impeccably in Prince Albert frock coats, gray dress vests, pin-striped trousers, pearl-gray spats over patent-leather shoes and high silk hats. That uniform was the trademark of Hamlin's Wizard Oil performers, and any man who appeared in public "out of dress," say in a roll collar instead of a wing collar, was promptly fined two dollars. Those outfits were the rule in the West, where a classy dresser was a rarity. In the Eastern states, where people were fascinated with the retreating frontiers of their nation, standard costume for the Hamlin pitchmen was Indian scout garb—a buckskin jacket.

A Hamlin's Wizard Oil unit might visit a town for two to six weeks. During that time, to promote local goodwill, the concert quartets were volunteered to sing in church choirs, at fairs or at charity bazaars. No false or high-pressure techniques were used to ballyhoo the medicine, because the Hamlin shows certainly wanted to come back. The main purpose was to place bottles of Wizard Oil, Cough Balsam and Blood and Liver Pills in stores along the way. A demand was created, and merchants reordered and restocked medicines every time the wagons came through. John A. and Lysander B. Hamlin had a solid business going for many years.

Gradually, toward the end of the nineteenth century, customers grew bored with the Indian shows, the same old war whoops, same old Indian dances; and a new gimmick had to be found to sell medicine on the road. Jim Ferdon came up with a great idea, the Quaker Medicine Company. Anybody would trust a Quaker doctor, he reasoned.

When Jim Ferdon was twelve years old in Litchfield, Illinois, Doc Jim Lighthall came to town flashing his diamonds and his strong personality. With Lighthall as hero and inspiration, Jim Ferdon determined to make his own place in the medicine show business, and his tale is a classic one of "country boy makes it to pitchman fame."

Ferdon started as a boy soprano, billed as the Boy Wonder, with a show run by one of Lighthall's former employees. At seventeen, now able to play the banjo and perform on the trapeze, Ferdon signed on with a Kickapoo Indian unit and served his apprenticeship under Nevada Ned Oliver. Soon he was off with another show to sell German Electric Belts, and before long his trademark song was, "I'm Electric Bill from over the hill; never worked and never will." After that he teamed with a Japanese to sell Chinese Herb Remedies.

And then he thought of the Quaker show idea; that was the beginning of the Big Time for Jim Ferdon. With a Dr. J. L. Berry he organized the Quaker Medicine Company and freely adopted Quaker dress and way of speaking. Ferdon and Berry and all their workers wore sober tan or gray clothing with Quaker-type hats, wide-brimmed and low-crowned; they spoke gently, saying "thee," "friend"; they never swore. People of the Quaker religion had a reputation for being honest, peaceful and God-loving; therefore, a pitch doctor who called himself a Quaker took on an air of religious honesty, and his medicine was accepted as trustworthy.

The entertainment in Ferdon's show was said to be too lively to bear any resemblance to the nearly silent Quaker religious meetings, but the public was delighted with this new approach to selling medicine. Mainly that medicine was a preparation of healing salts, which Dr. Berry said he had distilled from mineral springs in Death Valley, California. There was a marvelous tale of how prospectors in the Panamint Range had discovered the mineral springs, of how one drink cured them of chronic indigestion from an unbroken diet of sourdough bread and sourbelly pork.

The Quaker Medicine Company traveled as far as the Hawaiian Islands in 1898 and made a fortune for Jim Ferdon. Investing his

Other showmen and medicine makers imitated Jim Ferdon and his original Quaker Medicine Company. Bitters was a kind of tonic made up of powdered bitter roots, often dissolved in alcohol.

money in Los Angeles real estate, he became a wealthy man, and his Hollywood home was a showplace in the late 1920s. But Ferdon never gave up the road entirely. As late as 1928 he was the Great Pizzaro, touring Pennsylvania Dutch country with a black minstrel troupe.

After the Quaker Medicine Company—and its inevitable imitators—came the Shaker Medicine Company. But there was a difference. The Shaker people at Lebanon, Pennsylvania, really did supply the formulas for the medicines and kept a careful watch on the activities of the advertising troupes. William Burt, a showman who sang in a "Lyceum Four" quartet for Hamlin's Wizard Oil and lectured for the Big Sensation Medicine Company, also worked as a lecturer for a Shaker unit in the summer of 1893. Reminiscing in an article for *Colorado Magazine* in 1942, he said that the only entertainers were psalm singers dressed in Shaker bonnets and gowns of Shaker brown. The lecturers too were in Shaker brown, button-to-the-neck frock coats and bell-crowned hats. As the entertainment was low-key, Burt said the lecturers had to be top-notch pitch artists in order to sell. Burt's unit followed the medicine trail to the Rocky Mountains and played eighteen weeks in the Colorado Front Range towns—Pueblo, Colorado Springs, Denver and Boulder.

The traveling medicine show seldom penetrated the mountains of the Western United States. That shows did at all, considering three feet of snow on winter roads and mudholes and rocks on summer roads, is a tribute to the medicine man's dedication to tracking down a customer. "Your Uncle Dutchey" made it to Manti, Utah, in the early 1880s, according to the recollections of a Utah pioneer. He came in a brightly colored wagon, and the show troupe totaled four: two men who played banjos and sang, plus Dutchey and another man who sold their Vigor of Life. "Your Uncle Dutchey" made up to the children and did sleight-of-hand tricks, including one of eating cotton, which trick was imitated around Manti for years after. Another amazing trick was the way Uncle Dutchey seemed to run out of medicine to sell each night, so that the crowd would have to come back the next night to buy more medicine and hear new songs and jokes.

In 1872, Dr. Haskell mounted the Colorado Rockies as far as Central City in the Front Range. The *Central City Register-Call* reported in July:

> Dr. Haskell, the irrepressible and really one of the most amusing public speakers in the electric oil and patent medicine trade, kept a large assemblage in roars of laughter all the evening, and while the mirth was upon them, sold his wonderful preparations for the extinction of all the ills the flesh is heir to. The whole embellished with music from Brown's banjo. And by the way, this Brown is a "peeler" in his line, a capital vocalist and one of the most skillful performers on the banjo in the Union.

As the medicine show traveled into the twentieth century, joyously ballyhooing, enthusiastically spieling, the small-time medicine man continued to tour the rural areas in his buggy. Typical of those was Dr. Sloat, in frayed Prince Albert coat and rumpled trousers, offering his Magic Medicine to the tune of Civil War marching songs in Iowa villages.

But the showman with ambition for large sales offered a much wider variety of entertainment, actually a traveling vaudeville show so big it was carried from town to town by railway cars. Such big-time shows were the Big Sensation Medicine Company and the Ton-Ko-Ko Medicine Show. They played under canvas tents or at the local opera house and charged a small admission fee. William Burt lectured for Big Sensation for a while in Nebraska, and he reported a tent 60 x 120 feet, with 500 folding canvas chairs facing the stage and seats for 1000 in bleachers behind. Entertainment included actors, a twelve-piece brass band and the huge King of Forceps practicing "painless dentistry" on the stage. The Ton-Ko-Ko show, masterminded by Dr. J. W. Wellington, offered a noontime

Ox-drawn medicine wagon on a Denver, Colorado, street.

parade and free concert by the band in the town square, and on the stage in the evening were strong-man acts, comedy skits, fire-eaters, song-and-dance performers, even an excellent ballet dancer.

Until the late 1920s, the big shows prospered. Then gradually they became smaller, and in the 1930s their tours were confined mainly to the rural areas of the South and the Midwest. People just weren't buying the medicine the way they once did. Federal laws restricted the medicine man from making exaggerated claims for his remedy; magazines and newspapers were educating people about the actual health hazards in certain patent medicines; and other kinds of entertainment were available to country people— radio shows and the movies. During World War II in the 1940s, gasoline was rationed frugally to civilians, because of the increased need for fuel for military purposes. The shortage of gasoline restricted the few remaining medicine shows from travel by truck and car. By the 1950s so few medicine showmen still kept to the road that a small medicine show traveling in Missouri was reported as a rarity.

One last burst of excitement in medicine show business came in 1950, when Hadacol flooded the South and made a fortune for Dudley J. LeBlanc. LeBlanc, a Cajun who became a Louisiana state senator, went out behind his barn and in big barrels mixed up a concoction strong on B-complex vitamins. The murky brown tonic also included iron, calcium and honey on a base of 12 percent alcohol. LeBlanc promoted the tonic with newspaper advertisements, radio jingles and Hadacol jokes, and in the last two months of 1949 he spent over $300,000 on his massive advertising campaign. The next year he ballyhooed Hadacol with a gigantic medicine show that toured 3800 miles of the South, and a reported average of 10,000 fans bought a bottle of Hadacol each night as admission to the show. The entertainment must have been worth the price: steam calliopes, a Dixieland band playing "Hadacol Boogie," Chicago bathing beauties and top performers such as Roy Acuff, Mickey Rooney and George Burns and Gracie Allen.

But by then people could also hear those performers on the radio. They had cars to drive in from the farm to see Mickey Rooney in a movie. Television was coming.

"It was radio, autos and television that killed the medicine show," Cliff Mann said. "Those good old farmers, they didn't need us entertainers anymore."

Was that it? Did people buy the Vigor of Life and the Herbs of Joy out of gratitude for a free show? Maybe. Many a customer likes to get something for nothing. Maybe not. We need to look at the central figure, the medicine show doctor. Because it was at the end of his sales pitch that the farmer opened his wallet and bought that tonic. For one hundred years, medicine salesmen carried their shows around the United States and earned a living, sometimes a handsome living, by persuading people to buy their medicines. How did they do it?

4
THE PITCH
How Did They Do It?

Prince Nanzetta, Silk Hat Harry, Brother Jonathan, Ray Black, the Diamond King, Princess Lotus Blossom—fabled medicine men of the early twentieth century, and the queen of pitch doctors. After the ballyhoo, in the midst of the entertainment, it was their spiel that convinced people, who usually had no dollars to spare, to buy their medicine. How did they do it?

"My uncle and my dad were con artists, the way they ran their show," Cliff said.

And what is a con artist? One who deceives, who dupes?

Webster's Seventh New Collegiate Dictionary defines *con*: "1. swindle; 2. coax, cajole." And *cajole* is defined: "1. to persuade; 2. to deceive with soothing words or false promises."

As a con artist, the pitch doctor may have *swindled* and *deceived* in varying degrees, but his emphasis was on *coaxing, cajoling* and *persuading.*

In the largest sense, a con artist is anyone who cunningly persuades another—to anything. Generally, though, money or some kind of advantage results for the one who does the conning. He or she gains a person's confidence, misrepresents a product or an investment deal and then swindles the victim out of his money, whether a quarter or thousands of dollars. One who swindled through false promises came to be called a confidence man.

Professional confidence men and women have always operated wherever they find trusting or gullible people. Usually the friendly stranger smooth-talks a plausible story and offers something for nothing: an investment that will triple the "mark's" money, a product at a bargain price, a repair service for half the regular price, or a generous reward for assisting the stranger. One con game, the Pigeon Drop, has many variations, but basically, a stranger says he has found some money and the "pigeon" shall share in it, if only he will place an equal amount of money with a "lawyer" as security, until the found money legally can be released. The gullible victim withdraws money from the bank, and the friendly stranger disappears with the money.

For example, the Spanish Trunk swindle has been around for a long time, and I remember how excited my father was in the 1930s, when he received a letter about the trunk. The letter writer claimed to be a man, friendless and without relatives, who was being held in a Mexican jail for nonpayment of his debts. However, he owned a trunk full of Spanish gold that was being held in customs at the border until baggage charges were paid. The writer asked that $1000 be mailed to him to claim the trunk and get out of jail, and then the loan would be repaid tenfold in gratitude. Fortunately, my father did not have $1000 to forward to Mexico. Nowadays the asking price for redeeming the Spanish trunk is $50,000, according to a recent Denver newspaper article on con games.

Today's con artists are so active that major cities in the U.S. maintain in their police departments check, bunco and fraud divisions dedicated to tracking down or thwarting the swindlers.

The medicine showman was a con artist in that he gained people's confidence, and he often misrepresented his product, the medicine. But in contrast to the hit-and-run swindler, the medicine showman worked to make himself, his medicine and his free show so acceptable to customers that they were glad to see him come back, year after year.

The pitch doctor's art was in understanding human nature. In his sales pitch he appealed to the basic human reactions: anxiety about health, greed, curiosity, impulse under mass excitement, even goodwill—and always, credulity, readiness to believe out of lack of knowledge and experience.

Some showmen seemed to work a bit of hypnotism, too. Doc Bartok, who ran the big brassy Bardex show in the 1930s, spoke of the hypnotic pendulum technique. A good pitchman moved back and forth and from side to side as he talked, focusing the customer's attention and soothing him into the spieler's rhythm.

It was a matter of autosuggestion, Nevada Ned Oliver declared. The customer hypnotized himself. In 1929, in two *Saturday Evening Post* articles, Oliver reminisced about his medicine show days and stated the formula a pitch doctor learned to follow to make a sale:

> First, attention; second, interest; third, suggestion; fourth, imagination; fifth, desire; sixth, decision. It is a wise salesman who knows enough to stop talking at the decision signal on the faces of his push. With the gentlemen of the keister or platform this is termed "making the joint." Follows the Hurry-Up of the band, words, gestures and a constant reiteration of "A gentleman over here takes two bottles; this lady will try the remedy." Suggestion, auto-suggestion.

In the world of itinerant peddlers there was the High Pitch and the Low Pitch, but High and Low had nothing to do with the skill of the medicine showman. A High Pitch lecturer worked from a platform, a stage in a tent or in a hired opera house. The Low Pitch worker spieled on street corners or vacant lots, and often his only props were a gasoline torch and his suitcase of wares set on a tripod table, called "keister and tripes" in the trade vernacular. And like an artist, each pitch doctor developed his own unique style, his special way of persuading his customers.

"Try just one bottle of my tonic and . . ." A pitch doctor spiels to a crowd, about 1900.

Take curiosity. One way to attract a crowd was to stimulate curiosity—the opening ballyhoo. Professor Balrod, who toured the Midwest selling Indian Root, began with mystery. When he first arrived in a small town, no one knew what he was up to. Suddenly at night he would appear in the town square, glowing with phosphorescent paint in the flare of green fire burning beneath the platform on which he was seated. On either side of the exotically dressed man, two swarthy youths began to beat kettledrums slowly. Green light flickered over the people on the stage as the villagers gathered to stare, yet Professor Balrod did not utter a word that night.

In next morning's daylight he was not to be seen, but his platform remained. The town was abuzz with excitement and curiosity: No one knew whether he was a magician—or a scissors grinder. The next night he appeared again in a burst of green fire. When a large crowd had gathered, he drew from the folds of his robe a single bottle of his "miraculous cure." Seated upright, rigid, he chanted a weird song to the beating of the drums, on and on, hypnotically, until— Suddenly the song broke off, the drums ceased. Silence, tense and thick.

Then, slowly, softly, Professor Balrod began to preach about the bottle he held up, the miraculous ease of pain it promised. Whether out of release from tension or belief in the tonic, some villager always bought that first bottle. The Professor would produce another from a hidden place, and the sale was on. He never displayed more than one bottle at a time while he lectured, for he reasoned that a man will more likely buy if he thinks supply is short.

Another master of the art of teasing the curiosity was Ray Black, who worked the street corners and vacant lots in the early part of the twentieth century. He used a human skull, a big black Bible and a length of hempen rope. First he set up a folding table and placed on it his satchel of medicine. Then on the ground nearby he laid out the skull, the Bible and the rope. Paying no attention to the curious people beginning to gather, Ray Black arranged and rearranged his objects. The skull in front of the Bible, rope wrapped around . . . He stood back and studied the effect. Skull atop the Bible, rope coiled in front . . . Black worked with the display as if he were alone in the world.

At last, when a glance assured him he'd attracted a large-enough audience, Black would face the people and go into his medicine lecture. Yet he might never mention or explain the skull, the Bible and the rope. They were simply his come-on.

Ray Black was a "kidney man." He emphasized the symptoms and dangers of kidney trouble, and his spiel was admired in the trade as being the longest in medicine show business. Some claimed he could hold a crowd for up to five hours with his lecture. As Ray Black said, "If they stay with me until the end, they're sure to buy. By then the yokels' heels are round, their backs are aching from standing, and they are sure they have kidney trouble."

And then he offered relief. For one dollar, each man could buy a box of crystals brought from a magical spring in Australia, where Black himself had seen beautiful birds reputed to live five hundred years. By the time Black had spun out his tale of the marvels of his medicine, the customers were ready to buy. Actually, the crystals were said to be made from Epsom salts with a little flavoring added to disguise the taste.

The Diamond King exploited people's curiosity and greed, but what he depended on for his big money was people's goodwill. Here's how he worked his con game in San Antonio, Texas, in 1886:

One fine day he breezed into town dressed in diamonds. His Mexican sombrero was sprinkled with diamonds, his coat and vest were embroidered with diamonds, every sleeve and vest button was a big fat diamond. His servants told the astounded populace that the sparkling man was a diamond king. What's more, the great man would have something to say to the people on the following night at eight o'clock. Then the Diamond King, his wife and his servants disappeared into a tent they had erected near Alamo Plaza.

The next night not only the crowd's curiosity but its greed was rewarded. The Diamond King strode out of the tent and began throwing money to the people. Out of a sack flew dimes, quarters, dollars, even ten-dollar bills, and the people pounced and scrambled after the money. When the Diamond King, glittering in the torchlight, had convinced the crowd that he was a great benefactor, he shouted for attention. Holding aloft a bottle, he announced, "More important than money, I have discovered the most precious boon to mankind—a real painkiller!"

He rubbed an old woman's jaw with the painkiller to demonstrate, then pulled her sore tooth. No pain! His Spanish Oil was a miracle medicine! ("Miraculous" painkillers of that time often contained drugs such as opium.) Next day the Diamond King pulled teeth for one dollar apiece, tossing out more coins and bills between extractions. People thronged to buy the marvelous Spanish Oil.

But selling medicine was the penny-ante part of the Diamond King's gig. Next, word spread from Alamo Plaza that the wonderful man had died of smallpox. Oh, the poor widow! Her husband had given away to the people all of his money, even money he had borrowed on the diamonds. And the widow could not sell his diamond-studded clothing, because it was contaminated with smallpox.

People of goodwill flocked to donate hundreds of dollars for the relief of the widow, in sympathy for her bereavement and in gratitude to her generous-hearted husband.

Late at night behind the closed tent flap, the Diamond King and his wife counted up the donations. Then it was, "All right, dearie, we've cleaned up four thousand dollars in this town. Let's hit the road."

The only trouble with the Diamond King's act was that he could never go back.

Brother Jonathan used a ploy that assured he was welcome in a town. Although he called himself as well as his medicine "Giver of Life," he never antagonized local doctors when he brought his big show to new territory. Instead, he would become ill and summon several physicians to consult on his condition. He would declare that despite his years of medical research, "I have the utmost faith in my fellow physicians." The statement would appear in the local newspaper, and the doctors loved him. An impressive man with a drooping mustache, dressed in large hat and dark well-tailored suit, Brother Jonathan walked out in each town, swinging his gold-headed ebony cane, and first called on the mayor to pay his respects, then made a set list of purchases from local merchants. He depended on his dignified, compelling personality to win the public —although in private, as Jonathan Maloney, he talked the underworld argot, calling police informers "narks" and referring to writing a letter as "flying a kite."

Brother Jonathan's public image was the epitome of the medicine showman as grand old gentleman, skilled in the use of language, who could quote fluently from the Bible and Shakespeare. He claimed the great people of the 1890s as his personal friends, glibly name-dropping and telling anecdotes of his experiences with President Grover Cleveland and John L. Sullivan, the champion boxer. Behind the scenes, Brother Jonathan was an astute businessman. He ran a big show with vaudeville acts that included ventriloquists and magicians as well as the usual comedians, singers and dancers. All his employees were expected to perform impeccably offstage as well as on—"no boozers or woman-chasers," his ads for workers ran— and he was quick to fine anyone who behaved improperly.

Brother Jonathan's pitch was respectability. His grandly rolling lecture emphasized the worthiness of his medicines with Biblical quotations, gradually building up to "I come to you as one who bears the balm of Gilead out of Judea. . . . My medicine encircles the world. . . . Children cry for it! The friend of the family! The Giver of Life!"

Every week Brother Jonathan sent the profits from his show to his bank, and he was counted as one of the richest of medicine showmen.

His medicine consisted mainly of water, Epsom salts and powdered rhubarb. Yet people in the audience must have looked up at him and thought, *How could such an impressive man stand right up there and tell lies? It must be true about the medicine—I sure hope it's true.*

Little wonder if the farmer was amazed by the "health facts" delivered in a high-blown lecture by a salesman on the street corner. In the nineteenth and early twentieth centuries, people were more easily deceived about medicine because they had scanty access to factual medical information. Their schools did not teach details about the human body or how to maintain its health. Nor did magazines and newspapers make a habit of publishing articles on physical health, as they do today. Most people knew little about the internal makeup of their bodies or why their bodies "got out of whack," as they might term disorder. Lacking knowledge, many people feared being cut by the surgeon's knife, and many believed that a person went to a hospital only to die.

Instead of going to professional doctors, country people depended a good deal on folk-medicine advice passed along by word of mouth: "If you get a nail in your foot, wrap your foot in a rag soaked in coal oil to prevent lockjaw." "Put snuff on red-ant bites." "Turpentine will heal almost any sore."

A study of this nineteenth-century dependence on folk medicine, *The Midwest Pioneer: His Ills, Cures and Doctors*, tells that at times of illness many people were likely to obtain home-brewed remedies from a neighbor who specialized in herb medicine. And some of

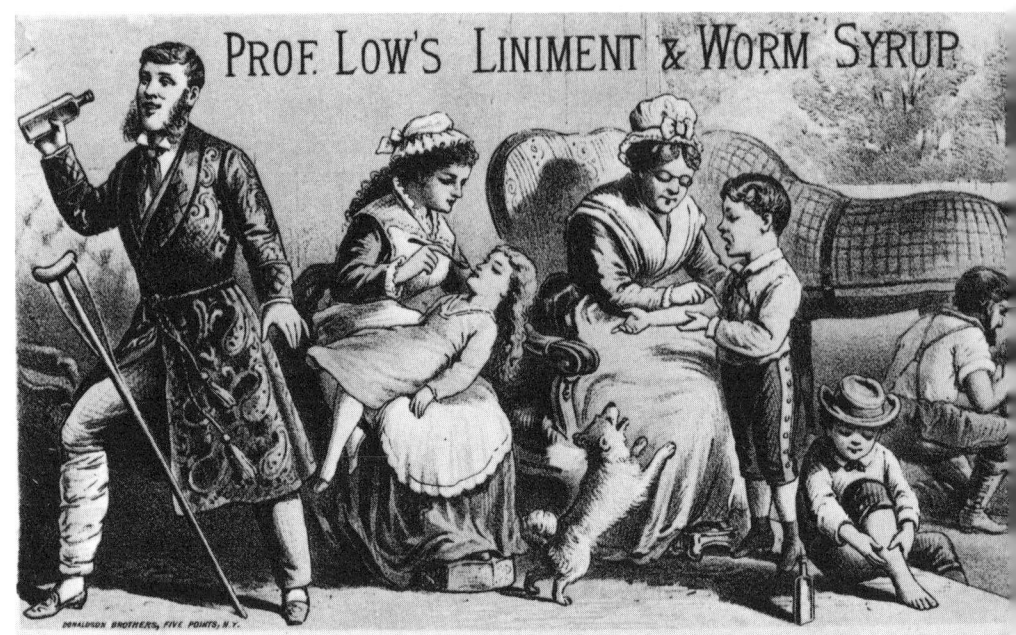

An advertisement for a syrup, supposedly a cure-all for many different ailments in men and beasts.

those wilderness healers dealt in supernatural medicine. They claimed "the power" to heal and mixed in a bit of white magic, with chants and laying on of hands. Superstitions about cures were many, and there was an aura of mystery about what went on inside the body.

Therefore, if the showman offered a folk medicine that was mysterious enough, exotic enough, people were eager to believe it could be a miraculous cure-all. Two who specialized in elaborate tales of mystery medicines from faraway lands were Prince Nanzetta and Princess Lotus Blossom.

At the age of eighteen a Mexican boy from Los Angeles went into the medicine show business and became Prince Nanzetta. He appeared on the streets in an eye-catching costume—a long crimson robe trimmed with gold thread and flashing with tiny mirrors. At his side he wore a short sword encased in ivory, and around his neck hung a chain bearing a great seal inscribed with Chinese characters. He was a royal prince of Tibet, he claimed, and he brought from that far-off mountain-locked country an ancient miracle medicine.

Prince Nanzetta's pitch-tale went like this: When he was a boy, he traveled with his father deep into the Himalayan Mountains on an expedition. Their party was captured by natives and all were slain except for the boy. Because of his youth he was accepted to be trained as a slave to the High Priests in the hidden city of Lhasa. There he became so skilled in the art of medicine, as taught by the priests he served, that at last they made him a prince. They hoped he would become one of their exalted clan, thinking and living as a Tibetan. But Prince Nanzetta remembered his ailing countrymen, and he escaped through a mountain pass, bearing the secret formula to heal his own people. . . .

Prince Nanzetta's act was so well believed that once, it is said, he sat on the platform with visiting dignitaries at a national political rally.

Several women achieved success at pitching medicine, among them Princess Iola from Quincy, Illinois, who sold complexion soap, and Madame Du Bois, who pulled teeth and sold medicine from a chariot. But the most colorful pitchwoman of them all seemed to be Princess Lotus Blossom. In later life she sold herb medicines under the name of Madame V. Pasteur; and after that, under her real name, Violet McNeal, she wrote a book rich in medicine show lore, *Four White Horses and a Brass Band.* She started life as Violet, a Midwestern farm girl who met up with a pitch doctor when she first moved to the big city of St. Paul, Minnesota, at the turn of the century. She married him, he taught her a mind-reading act, and soon Violet was learning the medicine show business. She determined to become its queen.

Princess Lotus Blossom made her debut as a Chinese mandarin maiden in a colorful robe bought in St. Louis by her husband, Will, who masterminded the act. Her opening night was on a tavern-lined street in Grand Rapids, Michigan. Will, a distinguished-looking man also in a Chinese robe, first tied the blindfold over her eyes, and they went into their much-used mind-reading act. Then in skillful, measured phrases he ballyed and built up to "Gentlemen, I give you Princess Lotus Blossom!"

Will slipped off his Chinese robe, whispered to her, "Talk until I come back," and left to tour the taverns.

After the first panic at being left alone to lecture, Violet said, she remembered the thrill of power she had felt as a youngster when her contralto singing voice had moved people to the altar at revival meetings; she remembered Will's advice, "Let your voice throb." And she began her tale of the secret handed down in her family, the Orient's most miraculous medicine, Tiger Fat:

A visiting prince, taken on a tiger hunt by his mandarin host, was badly mauled by a tiger. The prince was near death when a Chinese physician ordered the tiger skinned and cut up. The pieces were boiled in a pot and rendered into a fat, which was anointed to the prince's grievous wounds. At once the prince's wounds healed, and he recovered to splendid health.

Princess Lotus Blossom's instant success at selling Tiger Fat must have been aided by her tale of a second Oriental wonder medicine, Vital Sparks, "God's Gift to MEN." Her voice dropped so low that listeners had to strain to hear, she held a dramatic pause as she said, "And so, gentlemen, those virtual—those virtual eunuchs cried, *Pong Wook-Eee!* at the return of their lost manhood."

Although the precious Vital Sparks were priced at five dollars a box, that night she would give away one box free with each one-dollar purchase of Tiger Fat. "I am not going to sell them tonight. I am going to *give* them away!" Something for nothing! The customers thronged to buy Tiger Fat.

Princess Lotus Blossom pitched in Oklahoma and Arkansas, on the streets of Los Angeles, San Francisco and Seattle, in the gold-mining camps of California and in many a smallish town of the intermountain West. She decked herself in diamonds and pawned them; she made a fortune and lost it. Violet never realized her dream of having four white horses and a brass band for her ballyhoo. But at one time her business was so thriving that she rented offices in a busy section of Seattle and kept hired lecturers working from nine A.M. until ten P.M. With the aid of entertainers, she and her pitchmen took turns lecturing on the sidewalk about medicine. Several times during her lecture Violet would invite customers to visit the office for a free consultation and advice. As she said, a sucker never did get over the idea that he might get something without paying for it. In the offices were men called casetakers, some of them actually doctors with diplomas, who would diagnose the customers' ailments. As the cure, the casetaker always prescribed taking a long course of Violet's medicine, which meant the customer purchased a large supply.

By the time she was in her twenties, Violet was experienced at manipulating human nature. One thing she understood was that she couldn't persuade a crowd that was scattered. The people needed to be packed in so close that their noses were fairly touching the platform, she said. Yet if she asked them to step in a little closer, they might shy away warily. Animals were often a part of the opening ballyhoo, and Violet used hers carefully. It was a Gila monster. After the performers had attracted a crowd, Violet would take the Gila monster from a satchel and hold it up, calling attention to the beautiful beaded markings on the lizard's body. The venom had been removed from the lizard she called Gus; otherwise, when he bit, the venom would flow from grooves beside his lower teeth.

"Now I am going to show you Gus's teeth," she would say.

Everyone pushed forward to see the exotic lizard's teeth—and there she had them, packed in close. Violet went on to say that the Gila monster was not only a beautiful reptile but useful, for scientists used its venom for nerve disorders. From *disorder* it was an easy step into her medicine pitch.

Gus died eventually, but Violet kept the Gila monster on ice in a saloon icebox and displayed him nightly until she could get a replacement from Texas.

Although the Queen of Medicine Shows was clever and beautiful, some of her success must have been a result of following her famous dictum: "Never doctor a sick man, and never, never doctor a woman, sick or well." Women were harder to fool than men, she declared, and more likely to make trouble if they thought they'd been swindled.

Doubt in a customer's mind always was to be forestalled. Each pitch doctor's performance was gauged step by step to prepare the customer for that moment of decision when he was persuaded to buy the medicine. Charles S. Mundell, a pitchman who was also a writer, gave his version of those important steps in an article in the *Haldeman-Julius Monthly* in 1925.

That year Mundell and his partner, Doc James Heady, sold

medicine in San Francisco in a Market Street store building. In order to attract the attention of people passing by, Mundell would draw pictures on a blackboard on the sidewalk in front of his store, all the while telling jokes about the drawings. Often he had hired one or two men to watch him, thus forming the nucleus of a crowd. When enough people had stopped to watch and listen, gradually Mundell would back into the hall with his blackboard, bringing his audience with him. Inside he mounted a platform and switched his chatter from light entertainment to a health lecture.

Mundell said in his article:

> The secret of the pitchman's art (and it is an art) is to make the "switch" so subtly, so imperceptibly, and so scientifically, that he holds his crowd and carries them along with him. The "switch" is the pitchman's danger line. The least slip or bungle, and his crowd may get wise and walk out on him. . . .
>
> He talks anywhere from an hour to an hour and a half, playing upon the hopes and fears, the aches and pains, the ignorance and lack of information of his hearers, as dextrously as a harpist plays upon the strings of his instrument, until they are unconsciously "sold" before they hardly realize what it is all about.
>
> The second critical moment in the pitch-game, the "zero hour" of the ballyhoo artist, is the "close," when his goods are offered for sale.
>
> The wise medicine man always provides for this contingency by arranging for three or four shills to be the first to step forward and buy. These shills may be hired from the ranks of the unemployed in any large city, at from two to three dollars per day.

Mundell said he and Heady took in four to five hundred dollars a week, selling Doctor Heady's Peerless Remedy and Indian Herbs.

If a few persons could be hired to start the buying, the crowd would become infected by the mass excitement of buying the miracle cure.

"All sold out, Doctor!" was the rallying cry of that mass excitement in medicine shows from the Kickapoo days in the 1880s to the Ton-Ko-Ko shows in the twentieth century. At that psychological moment when the medicine was offered for sale, young men with baskets of bottles would circulate through the audience. On stage the Indians pounded their drums, or a brass band burst into fast music, and the young men set up a din of shouts: "Another bottle sold!" "More medicine, Doctor!" "All sold out, Doctor!" Of course, they carried a limited supply in their baskets and had to keep dashing back to the stage for more bottles, generating more noise and excitement. At the cry "All sold out!" men were said to fight through the crowd toward a salesman who still had a bottle or two in his basket. In some Quaker shows the Healer would answer the all-sold-out cry with "Bless you, my friends!"

Shills to start that buying could be hired in cities, where people didn't know each other; but medicine showmen traveling the small towns could not depend on a rube not to tell his neighbors he'd been hired. Many pitch doctors relied only on their powers of persuasion to convince people to buy medicine.

Con, confidence, confidence man . . . Remember that High German Doctor who promoted his marvelous cures at a London fair in the eighteenth century? When he had finished his lecture, "The people laughed incredulously and yet believed every word . . . and began to push and shove each other in their eagerness to buy the wonderful medicines."

Believe is the key word. After a few years on the road, the best-known medicines, Kickapoo Indian Sagwa and Hamlin's Wizard Oil, had gained such widespread and good reputations that customers were predisposed to believe in their efficacy.

Sick people wanted to believe a medicine could help them; even more, they desired a sure cure, an absolutely effective remedy that would give them perfect health. From one standpoint, the nineteenth century might be called the age of the panacea—"the sure cure for all our troubles is . . ." And people must have been conditioned to believe in the possibility of a cure-all. *The answer to*

A medicine showman featuring an Indian ballyhoo.

all our troubles is public-school education for everyone, declared Horace Mann, crusading for school reform in the 1830s. (In fact, not all the states in the U.S. required public elementary school attendance until 1918, when Mississippi was the last state to pass a compulsory-school-attendance law.) *The answer to all our troubles is free public libraries,* declared other crusaders. *The answer is for everyone to stop drinking alcohol,* insisted Temperance leaders. *The sure way to stay healthy is to wear flannel next to the skin . . . to take steam baths . . . to eat graham flour* (unsifted wheat flour, named after Sylvester Graham, the dietary proponent whose name survives in our graham crackers) *. . . to sleep with the windows open, because otherwise there's not enough oxygen in the room.*

Troubles and ill health continued, but many people stayed hopeful of a cure-all and were ready to believe a person who styled himself an authority. The smart medicine showmen worked on that readiness to believe.

At the turn of the century, Doctor Punja used the progression of logic to establish belief. Calling himself a Hindu doctor, he lectured on the wonders of nature. In his sideshow tents he exhibited to people certain marvels: "Siamese twins," a "petrified man." As Doctor Punja pointed out, the people would not believe such wonders existed if they could not see them with their own eyes. Yet wonders did exist, and here was a wonder of nature to heal people —his marvelous Indian Elixir!

His lecture concluded in this fashion: "You need not take my word for it. A trial will convince you. Is it not worth a dollar to make the trial? I ask you, is it not worth a dollar?"

Many a small-town man who had not known a "petrified man" existed before that night did indeed believe the miracle cure was worth a dollar.

The old maxim "Seeing is believing" was often employed by showmen. Doc McDonald, Cliff Mann's Uncle Jude, worked it effectively to sell his tonic. On stage he would weigh a box painted black: 25 pounds—everyone could see that register on the scales. He invited men to come up to the stage and take turns lifting the box.

Cliff recalled that Jude would tell the men, "See how heavy it is to lift? Now you take my tonic. After a week on McDonald's Compound you come back, and you'll just see how much easier it is to pick up a twenty-five-pound box."

The tonic takers came back at the end of the week. Doc McDonald would weigh another box on the scales: 25 pounds exactly. And every man declared that box was easier to lift. The tonic had made them stronger! The only difference was that the second box was painted light green.

"I've done it myself," Cliff Mann told me, "and that light green box *was* easier to pick up than the black box. I never understood that until I went to art school and found out they call it 'color dynamics.' But people would come back, and they'd swear it was easier to pick up the twenty-five-pound box, and they'd load up on that tonic. Seeing is believing."

And many a customer must have believed the showman's claims, because parts of his statements about health and the body were true. The customer needed medical knowledge to sort out the truths and the falsehoods in Silk Hat Harry's lectures.

Silk Hat Harry was a famous pitchman—his was a nonsoap cleanser "saponified with soap bark that grows in the highest altitudes of Colorado"—who also specialized in the mineral salts lecture. Presumably he wore a silk top hat like a professor—or a magician. His assurance and his free-flowing discussion of the body's ails often were sufficient to command the belief of the most cynical of his street customers. Because there would be half-truth in what he said. And the customer generally had only half-knowledge.

Violet McNeal, in her book, quoted how Silk Hat Harry would spiel: "Now the first part of your body that breaks down is the stomach." Many middle-aged customers know indigestion and stomach trouble intimately. They peer at the diagram of a stomach that Silk Hat Harry holds up. "Now in three minutes I'll tell you all about your stomach." He dwells on the symptoms of stomach trouble and their supposed cause, then moves on to the liver. "Now in five minutes you're going to know all you'll ever need to know about your liver. The first stage of disease of the liver is that backache that hits so many of you right across the small of your back." Plenty of those potential customers have suffered backaches, too.

With knowledgeable words and impressive delivery, the lecturer details the actions and failures of the liver. "The kidneys . . . uric acid," he says. That seems to check—uric acid has something to do with the kidneys. "The famous mineral springs in the mountains, that's where the rich people go to take the mineral waters that neutralize the uric acid in their systems." True, rich people go to the mountain resorts to take the waters, but the members of the audience can't afford—

"So I have brought the mineral springs to you! I have distilled those very same mineral-water salts and placed them in bottles. See the gleaming, health-giving salts!

". . . take in a glass of water nightly. Only fifty cents a bottle. Who'll—"

"Over here, Harry! I'll take two!"

The pitch doctor has played on the potential customer's anxiety about health; he has stimulated the customer to imagine a marvelous cure; he has turned need into desire for his product; he has convinced the customer to believe his half-truths about the body, the ailment and his medicine. He has made a sale.

5
THE AILMENTS AND THE MEDICINE
"Now I Bring You This Miraculous Cure!"

"Shoot, all that was the matter with most of those farmers was calluses and constipation," said Cliff Mann.

It is a fact that medicine shows became known in the trade as "physic shows," because so many of their wonder cures were laxatives. True, most pitch doctors salved their consciences by declaring that at least they sold good physics. And true, they were pursuing an old medical tradition: Until the middle of the nineteenth century, many of the best physicians prescribed purging the body of "poisons." No wonder purgative patent medicines claimed to cure such diverse ailments as rheumatism, ague and fever, measles, toothache and epidemic cholera.

But constipation was not the cause, nor purging the solution, for the major ailments that early Americans suffered, such as yellow fever, malaria, typhoid fever, tuberculosis and hookworm. Yellow fever, brought up from the West Indies by infected persons, struck again and again in epidemics in New York City, Boston, Philadelphia and elsewhere at the end of the eighteenth century. Malaria, also called ague and fever ("fevernager"), was common from the Eastern seaboard to the Mississippi River Valley, as generations of pioneers took the disease westward in their bloodstreams. Malaria ranged in virulence from fever-wracked death to chronic infection in weakened people who grimly took for granted the recurrent chills and shaking. They learned that quinine would control the symptoms and that somehow the disease was more prevalent in "sickly country"—swamplands—but they attributed it to the swamps' "bad air" (hence the word *malaria*). No one understood that the disease-bearing mosquito in the swamp was the link. No one knew that germs existed to cause the tuberculosis of the lungs they called consumption. Nor did medical science understand that infected streams and wells caused typhoid fever, commonly called bilious fever or the flux. Nor did doctors know that hookworms bred in filth and entered bare feet in the South to cause major debilitation of whole populations.

With a myriad of physical afflictions to combat and little medical knowledge to help them, pioneers seized on anything that might cure them. Some people would believe anything if they felt miserable enough and lacked accurate knowledge, and so in the nineteenth century folk-charm cures were popular: To prevent a backache, turn a somersault upon hearing the first call of a whippoorwill in spring. To cure whooping cough, hang around your neck a bag of live ground bugs; or drink white-ant tea; or wear a stolen blue ribbon; or if all those fail, pass the sufferer three times through a horse collar. A neighbor who claimed to have "the power" might try to cure erysipelas (runny sores) with magic words and a red thread. The white witch would give you an eyewash made of March snow and charm away the cataracts from your eyes by tying around your neck a bag made of never-washed cloth containing bread, salt and wheat.

And then there were the home-remedy books which many a housewife consulted. She doctored her family with concoctions listed in such books as *Symptoms and Treatment of All Disease*, printed in Cedarville, Ohio, in 1843. In that book, H. D. Mason prescribed for asthma: licorice squills, lobelia, skunk cabbage, coffee or a poultice of hops and flaxseed. He also suggested galvanism (small electric shocks), a treatment popular when electricity and its possible uses were still a novelty.

If Americans did trust themselves to a doctor in the first half of the nineteenth century, their treatment was generally one or a combination of three methods: bleeding, blistering and purging. Bloodletting was standard practice in most feverish conditions, on the theory that the body was too hot with blood—"bleed the man until he is faint and relaxed." To bleed a person, small incisions were made with a sharp-pointed, two-edged surgical instrument called a lancet. Suction cups were then applied to remove blood. Leeches (bloodsucking freshwater worms) also were commonly used to draw blood from patients; to encourage the leeches to take hold, the patient's skin might be spread with cream, sugar or blood.

Blistering poultices were applied to the skin in order to warm and irritate a part of the body. The poultice might contain mustard or a kind of beetle called the Spanish fly, ground and powdered, and the reddening of the skin showed the treatment was working.

Purging the "body's poisons" meant using a strong laxative, such as calomel and jalap mixed equally. (Calomel is a chemical formula of mercurous chloride; jalap is powdered from the dried root of a Mexican plant.) In the purging process an emetic of ipecac (powdered root of a South American plant) might also be administered to induce the patient to vomit.

Why did doctors administer such torturous treatments? Historian J. C. Furnas explains in *The Americans*:

> Medicine was still handcuffed by arbitrary theories inherited from the ancient and medieval worlds based on the principle that disease comes of imbalance among the humors (basic body elements), and the physician's task was to restore balance by dosage with violent drugs, bleedings and so on. Hence the probably needless death of George Washington in 1797. Still vigorous at the age of sixty-seven,

Col. T. A. Edwards, founder of the Oregon Indian Medicine Company. Its chief product, Ka-Ton-Ka, was a tonic advertised as made from roots gathered in Oregon by the Modoc and Nez Percé Indians. Other products were War Paint Ointment and Nez Percé Catarrh Snuff.

he caught cold and had doctors in. Conscientiously they weakened him by prolonged bleeding, then by calomel to purge his bowels and tartar emetic to make him vomit, then applied blistering poultices.

Faced with cures that often failed, or at the least felt worse than the ailments, many people did not trust doctors. As late as 1875, *Dr. Herrick's Almanac* was repeating the ironic anecdote about Rabelais, a sixteenth-century French satirist, who, lying on his deathbed and listening to the plans of his physicians, was supposed to have said, "Pray, let me die a natural death."

The people turned for help more and more to patent medicines: Lydia E. Pinkham's Vegetable Compound for Female Complaints. Ka-Ton-Ka and Nez Percé Catarrh Snuff from the Oregon Indian Medicine Company based in Corry, Pennsylvania. Dr. Pierce's Golden Medical Discovery and Doan's Kidney Pills, their ads painted on barn and fence across the nation.

Bitters, crushed and brewed from dewberry, wild cherry, yellow poplar or sumac, combined with hazel leaves, cider, whiskey or brandy—and the more bitter the brew tasted, the more effective it must be. Thirty brands of sarsaparillas, topped in sales by Ayer's and Hood's, taken faithfully in the spring as a purifier to "eliminate poison from the blood and tissues." Minard's Liniment, "the great internal and external remedy for man or beast." Smart's Rheumatic and Neuralgic Paste, "made from the Oil of Angle Worm, Cayenne Pepper, Frogs and Gum Camphor. . . . It will cure Toothache, Nervous Headache, Neuralgia, Pains in the Back, Chilblains . . . Catarrh."

And of course, the many products of the Kickapoo Indian Medicine Company: Indian Sagwa, Kickapoo Indian Prairie Plant (for Female Complaints), Kickapoo Indian Oil, Salve ("made from Buffalo Tallow, Combined with Healing Herbs and Barks"), Cough Cure, Pills and Worm Killer, all compounded from tribal formulas. The Kickapoo Indian Oil is supposed to have had a heavy

Sarsaparillas were popular as spring tonics, and Hood's Sarsaparilla was a leader in sales, with its imaginative advertising.

Kickapoo Indian Salve, a popular item of the Kickapoo Indian Medicine Company, caught the attention of customers with this dramatic scene.

proportion of camphor, and the Cough Cure's ingredients included Jamaica rum and New Orleans molasses.

The flood of tonics, pills, salves and liniments grew until by the early 1900s the volume of the patent-medicine business had reached $80 million a year.

No wonder medicine shows did a thriving business! The ailing were inclined to buy a "miracle cure" from almost anyone. They bought from the vendors who showed up on court days, at political rallies or wherever a crowd assembled; they bought from the traveling medicine shows; increasingly they bought their patent medicines from the shelves of the drugstores and the country general stores; they even bought their tonics by mail order.

The 1902 Sears, Roebuck catalogue listed twenty pages of medicines, such as the Mexican Headache and Neuralgia Cure and the White Ribbon Secret Liquor Cure. The Heidelberg Electric Belt, recommended for "the relief and cure of all chronic and nervous diseases . . . peculiar to men," sold for eighteen dollars. Vin Vita —Wine of Life—at sixty-nine cents a bottle, was "not a medicine, not merely a stimulant, but a genuine toner and strengthener . . . made with South American herbs. . . ."

Any concocter might apply the word *patent* to his proprietary medicines, whether homemade or factory-stirred. To the unknowing customer, *patent* implied government sanction, maybe even recommendation. Yet at the most, *patent* meant that the trade name was registered.

A few responsible journalists tried to warn people to beware of nostrums. In 1824 an editor spoofed in the *Portsmouth* (Ohio) *Journal*: "Dr. Balthasar Beckar respectfully informs the public that he is possessed of the genuine ABRACADABRA and understands the true use of the Dandelion flower. . . . He is the inventor of a PILL that will straighten a Roman nose into Grecian. . . ."

In 1897 a Chicago man, W. A. Ballard, was publishing a monthly magazine, *The Medical Investigator*, dedicated to exposing "Medical Fraud and Charlatanism." He listed the formulas for certain proprietary medicines and designated them *safe* or *dangerous.* "Humbug!" Ballard called the claims of one medicine company. "Men . . . unworthy to associate with the respectable portion of humanity." He warned against companies that made free offers, something for nothing. After blasting medical quacks and frauds, Ballard editorialized, "My advertising columns are open to all respectable advertisers."

And yet, and yet . . . On the back page of *The Medical Investigator* there is a Kidney and Bladder advertisement for the "Wonderful Kava-Kava Shrub" which will "drain the poisonous uric acid from the blood. . . . It costs you nothing. We send a large case by mail *free* to prove its power." And then, in a large advertisement on the same page, Ballard, the editor, proclaims, "YOUR RUPTURE CAN BE CURED." Ballard can do it by "fluid injection." He adds, "As this treatment is a sure cure, it should be given publicity, and our only object is philanthropy."

Whom do you trust?

Some trust anyone who speaks with authority. A doctor in Leadville, Colorado, must have known this when he advertised in 1880 that he could "change Colorado air into Boston air by means of an apparatus using electricity ozone" for the relief of those who could not stand the 10,000-foot altitude at Leadville.

At last the federal government put legal controls on the extravagant claims of medicine vendors and insisted they list on the labels the ingredients in the bottles. The action came as a result of exposés of the frauds and dangers in patent medicines published in *Ladies' Home Journal* in 1904 and *Collier's Weekly* in 1905. The *Journal* exposé was mainly concerned with Lydia Pinkham—long dead, although still purportedly answering letters—and her Vegetable Compound for Female Complaints. The series of articles in *Collier's* magazine, however, set forth the facts on everything crusading reporter Samuel Hopkins Adams could find out about

Medical frauds and charlatans are depicted as cockroaches in this cover drawing from The Medical Investigator, *July 1897.*

In 1905, crusading reporter Samuel Hopkins Adams published a series of articles in Collier's *magazine that aroused public feeling for the passage of the Pure Food and Drug Act in 1906.*

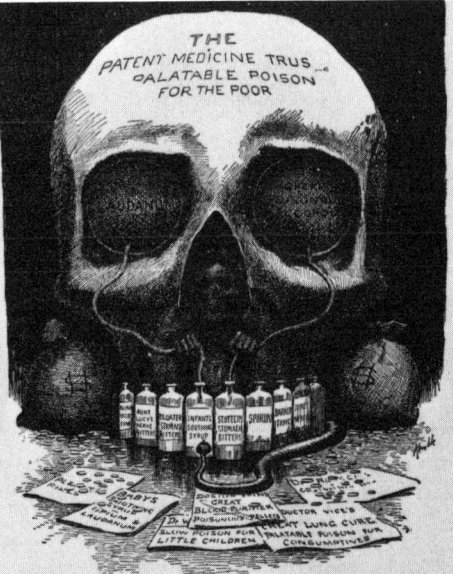

Death's Laboratory

Drawn by E. W. Kemble

COLLIER'S EXPOSÉ
OF THE
PATENT MEDICINE FRAUD

DEATH'S LABORATORY

June 3d

"Patent medicines are poisoning people throughout America to-day. Babies who cry are fed laudanum under the name of syrup. Women are led to injure themselves for life by reading in the papers about the meaning of backache. Young men and boys are robbed and contaminated by vicious criminals who lure them to their dens through seductive advertisements."

CRIMINAL ALLIANCE OF THE NEWSPAPERS WITH FRAUD AND POISON

July 8th

"Newspapers have done so much to create the success of 'fakes' in medicine that their duty is clearly to help remove them. It sounds high-minded for Journalism to bark ferociously against the reign of graft in politics or in high finance, but it can practice a little real reform, if it chooses, by canceling some of the most profitable results of its own limberness of conscience."

THE GREAT AMERICAN FRAUD

October 7th

"Gullible America will spend this year some seventy-five millions of dollars in the purchase of patent medicines. It will swallow huge quantities of alcohol, an appalling amount of opiates and narcotics, a wide assortment of varied drugs, ranging from powerful and dangerous heart depressants to insidious liver stimulants; and, far in excess of all other ingredients, undiluted fraud."

PERUNA AND THE "BRACERS"

October 28th

"So well recognized is the use of Peruna for its alcoholic effects that a number of Southern papers advertise a cure for the 'Peruna habit.' What makes Peruna profitable to the maker and a curse to the community at large, is the fact that the minimum dose first ceases to satisfy; then the moderate dose, and finally the maximum dose; and the unsuspecting patron, who began with it as a medicine, goes on to use it as a beverage, and finally to be enslaved by it as a habit."

CONSPIRACY AGAINST THE FREEDOM OF THE PRESS

November 4th

"So it was no mean intellect which devised the scheme whereby every newspaper in America is made an active lobbyist for the Patent Medicine Association. The man who did it is the present president of the organization; its executive head in the work of suppressing public knowledge, stifling public opinion, and warding off public legislation."

LIQUOZONE

November 18th

"Liquozone is sulphurous and sulphuric acids (corrosive poisons) heavily diluted; that is all. Will the compound destroy germs in the body? A series of tests conducted by the Lederle Laboratories answers the question in this summary: 'To summarize, we would say that *Liquozone had no curative effect*, but did, when given in pure form, lower the resistance of the animals so that they *died a little earlier than those not treated.*'"

THE SUBTLE POISONS

December 2d

"Nostrums there are which reach the thinking classes as well as the readily gulled. Depending as they do for their success upon the lure of some subtle drug concealed under a trade-mark name, or some opiate not readily obtainable under its own label, these are the most dangerous of all quack medicines, not only in their immediate effect, but because they create enslaving appetites, sometimes obscure and difficult of treatment; most often, tragically obvious. Of these concealed drugs, the headache powders are the most widely used."

Other Articles to be Announced Later

If you can not secure these issues from your dealer, they will be mailed to you on receipt of price, which may be sent in the form of stamps. Address P. F. COLLIER & SON, 430 West Thirteenth Street, New York City.

NEWSDEALERS EVERYWHERE

Collier's
THE NATIONAL WEEKLY

TEN CENTS PER COPY

patent medicines. He was horrified and angered by the amount of alcohol—as much as 47 percent—and drugs such as opium contained in the medicines sold for family use.

President Theodore Roosevelt was horrified, too. In 1906, despite the powerful patent-medicine lobby in Congress, the president signed the Federal Pure Food and Drug Act that became law on January 1, 1907. According to the law, the word *cures* could not be used on a medicine bottle label, only "for the relief of"—kidney trouble, rheumatism or whatever. Also, the label had to list the diseases for which the remedy was intended. No longer could a medicine showman claim his medicine was a "cure-all." And soon, with the Narcotics Act of 1914, the names and amounts of certain dangerous drugs, such as opium, cocaine, morphine and chloroform, were required by law to be listed on the label.

Yet many people still continued to buy patent medicines, so medicine shows continued to do a good business in the early part of the twentieth century. The showman obtained his wares from one of three sources: the mother factory, as in the case of the big companies like Kickapoo and Hamlin's Wizard Oil; drug manufacturing firms; or his own cupboard.

When Brother Jonathan mixed his Giver of Life compound in a large wooden tub, he dressed for the part. He wore a long white linen physician's coat, rubber gloves and a towel wrapped around his head. Going on the reasonable assumption that water is one of our most precious gifts of life, Brother Jonathan mixed a tonic that was three-fourths water. The other ingredients were Epsom salts, burnt sugar, powdered rhubarb, licorice powder and wintergreen essence.

Violet McNeal (Princess Lotus Blossom) told how she put together the Tiger Fat and the Vital Sparks. Although she bought her ingredients from conventional wholesale drug firms, her hotel room was her laboratory. To prepare Tiger Fat, Violet melted petroleum jelly in a large bucket. Into that she measured portions of camphor, menthol crystals, oil of eucalyptus, turpentine and oil of wintergreen. Stirring briskly, she added shavings of paraffin to set the mixture. While it was still warm, she poured it into small round tin boxes, stuck Tiger Fat labels on the lids, and the salve was ready for sale. Each tin of fat cost about seven cents to make and sold for one dollar—as the Oriental cure for eczema, ringworm, cold sores, burns and rheumatism.

Not a bucket but the hotel dresser drawer was needed for the manufacture of Vital Sparks—"God's Gift to MEN." Violet bought, by the barrel, a small hard black candy known as buckshot candy. She would pour a quantity of that into the bureau drawer, sprinkle it with water and shake the drawer back and forth until the candy was damp. Then she tossed a handful of powdered aloes on the damp candy and shook the drawer again until the black pellets were coated with the bitter aloes. Into cardboard boxes went the medicine labeled Vital Sparks.

Later, when Violet, as Madame V. Pasteur, prepared her herb remedies in the hotel bathtub, she complied with the new federal law that said: "All medicine must be packaged under the supervision of a registered pharmacist in sanitary quarters." Violet hired a drugstore clerk who was a registered pharmacist to come down to the hotel room while the medicine was being prepared. She always showed him the bottle of Lysol with which the bathtub had been washed. The herbs, which she had purchased in individual bags from drug firms, might include cascara bark, Cape aloes, sassafras and berberis root. It was a simple matter to empty the bags into the bathtub, mix up the powder by hand and spoon it into labeled tin boxes. "Eight to ten cents to make, for sale at one dollar a copy," Violet said.

The customer loved the gimmickry of medicine show sales, fancy names like Tiger Fat and shining displays of ferocious dental tools.

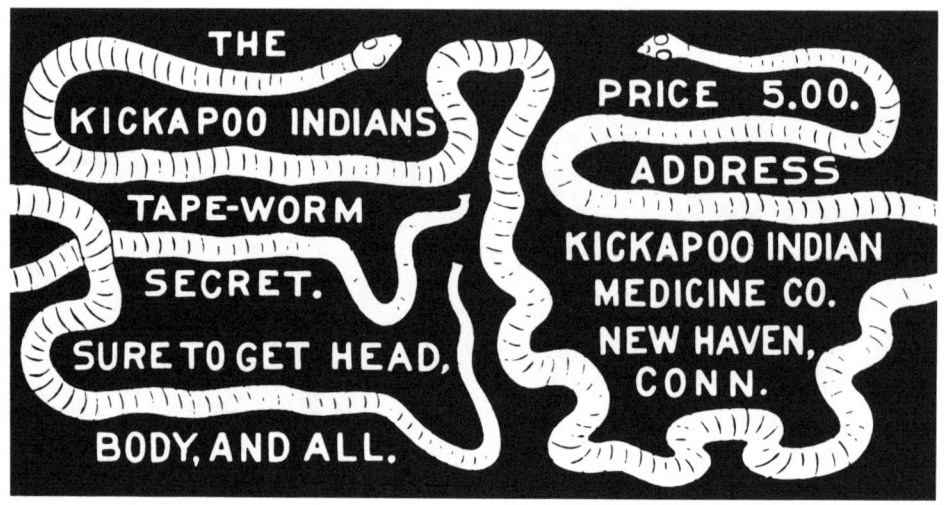

It seemed he would much rather buy an Oriental wonder medicine named Tiger Fat than a simple salve made of petroleum jelly.

Tapeworms were standard equipment for many a medicine show. A display of horrific long worms draped over wires in two-quart bottles, coupled with a lecture of the (common) symptoms of tapeworm, were guaranteed to frighten people into buying the cure. When the preparation sold by the pitch doctor actually did remove a tapeworm from a patient, the wondrous event was announced at the next night's show, both the doctor and the embarrassed customer exceedingly proud.

Liver pads sold well for many a huckster. Before starting the Kickapoo shows, John Healy sold liver pads with a touring wagon troupe happily named Healy's Liver Pad Concert Company. The pads might be touted as electric or galvanic, but generally their main ingredient was oil of capsicum—red pepper. The medicated pad was clamped over the pit of the stomach on the theory of absorption through the pores. Some said the pads were stuffed with sawdust treated to "smell like a drugstore," but certainly the pepper was there, and when warmed by the body's heat, the "gentle soothing warmth" and reddening of the skin meant the medication was taking effect. Liver pads or liniment, they had to burn to work.

"Painless" dentistry often was a sideline talent of the medicine showman. Cliff's Uncle Jude pulled teeth; the Diamond King pulled teeth to demonstrate his Spanish Oil; Violet, when she started out, pulled teeth. Whether the operation actually was painless is debatable. Some pitch doctors seem to have applied an opium-doped painkiller to the patient's mouth before extracting a tooth. In one showman's report, the orchestra's horns and drums played as loudly as possible during the tooth yanking, so that no outcry or groan from the patient could be heard by the audience.

One of the famous medicine show dentists billed himself as The King of Forceps. His wife was the Queen, and they both were so large that their combined weight was reported as close to 400 pounds. With the Queen holding the willing sufferer in a chair on the stage, and the King doing the yanking, no tooth, no matter how deepset, could resist. The royal pair traveled with the Big Sensation Medicine Company until misfortune struck: One time in a small Iowa town the King bore down too hard and broke a man's jaw. A lawsuit was filed against the King, and the show moved on without him.

Along with constipation and kidney trouble, catarrh was a favorite ailment the pitch doctor promised to cure—or relieve. Catarrh was the old-time name for the chronic irritation of the sinuses that causes mucous to run down the nose and drip in the throat, and many people who lived in the damp Ohio and Mississippi River valleys suffered from sinus trouble. Some medicine men claimed that the mucous poisoned the whole body. If the customer wasn't sure he had sinus trouble, the pitch doctor would convince him that he did.

Dramatic improvement is promised to sufferers of catarrh, Dr. Sage's remedy being one of many such cures offered for sinus trouble in the late 1800s.

Seeing is believing. When lecturing on catarrh, Violet, as Madame V. Pasteur, used a glass graduate filled with limewater, a glass drinking tube and a bit of vinegar in a bottle that supposedly contained the miracle medicine. Violet said her demonstration went like this:

"Now I will show you how V. Pasteur's Herbs will sweep the catarrh from your body. You, sir, do you have catarrh?"

"Nope, don't think so," declares the onlooker.

"Would you be willing to try . . . ?" The man is persuaded to step forward for the simple scientific experiment. Madame Pasteur explains to him and the attentive crowd that if the man has catarrh, the water in the glass graduate will turn milky when he blows into it. Taking the glass tube, the man bubbles the water vigorously, and according to its nature, the limewater clouds up.

"You have catarrh! Now see how the herbs treat your disease."

Violet pours the vinegar into the cloudy limewater and immediately the water clears. Sales thrive!

Good laxatives, purifying bitters, invigorating tonics, harmless herbs . . . But one wonders about the possible harmful effects of those medicines on the unknowing customer. How many persons treated their stomachaches with a "good laxative" sold by a pitch doctor and died of appendicitis? How many persons failed to seek medical treatment for major diseases because they were doctoring themselves with tonics?

The high alcoholic content of those invigorating tonics probably did produce a temporary feeling of well-being. And the tonics were popular in "dry" states, where liquor could not be purchased, so possibly not all the customers were unaware of the tonics' effects. But many a Temperance lady may have taken her daily dose of medicine without realizing she'd broken her pledge never to touch alcohol—Lydia E. Pinkham's Vegetable Compound for women was dissolved in 21 percent alcohol. The Temperance movement began in the early 1800s in the U.S., its members lecturing on the evils of drink and urging that the sale of alcohol be prohibited. Yet Temperance leaders and ministers, such as the famous preacher Henry Ward Beecher, were fooled into endorsing such alcohol-laden medicines as Bristol's Sarsaparilla, Hostetter's Celebrated Stomach Bitters and Dr. Hartman's Peruna, the latter widely advertised as a cure for catarrh. Hostetter's Bitters contained over 44 percent alcohol, and Peruna 28 percent, according to a chart published by reporter Samuel Hopkins Adams in his article on The Bracers, or alcoholic stimulators. The prescribed dosage of Peruna was three wineglassfuls to be taken in forty-five minutes. By contrast, table wine served nowadays contains about 12 percent alcohol.

In his angry exposé of the dangers of alcohol and drugs in patent medicines, Adams said most people with tuberculosis who had taken Peruna-type medicines showed a weakening of power to resist the disease, and many sufferers of typhoid fever masked their symptoms with those stimulants too long before going to a doctor.

In showing the effects of unsuspected drugs in patent medicines, Adams published a coroner's report that found that a two-year-old girl died from "the poisonous effects of opium, the result of drinking the contents of a bottle of Dr. Bull's Cough Syrup."

As for patent medicines advertised to cure drug addiction, Adams blasted their makers as "drug-cure fakers . . . who are men to do the work of Hell. The human wrecks made by the opium and cocaine habits come to them for cure, and are wrung dry of the last drop of blood." Adams discovered that a certain drug cure contained eleven grains of morphine, as much as an addict would consume in a day. Suggesting that some drug users had gained their addiction from patent medicines, Adams demanded that federal legislation require that the amount of habit-forming drugs in any medicine be listed on the label.

The Medical Investigator, the Chicago paper that published the elements of patent medicines in 1897, listed the formula for Birney's Catarrh Powder: Cocaine hydrochlorate, 19 gr., Magnesium pep-

Paine's Celery Compound was allegedly high in alcoholic content, a fact not generally known by those who endorsed it.

permint leaves, 18 gr., Powdered peppermint leaves, 5 gr., Sugar of milk, 1 oz. The *Investigator* added, "This is one of the most dangerous remedies on the market. Its tendency is to make cocaine fiends."

Nevada Ned Oliver of Kickapoo fame reported his horror at discovering he had acquired the cocaine habit while on an independent venture selling catarrh powder. He had been demonstrating the powder nightly, following the directions to blow the powder into the nostrils with a bulb. When his nose became inflamed and his nerves jumpy, he checked up on the ingredients of the powder and learned it was made of menthol, sugar of milk and cocaine. Oliver immediately closed the show and went home to Chicago in a panic. Before, he had used liquor only sparingly, but he now found it necessary to drink a pint or more of whiskey at night in order to sleep. Only by great willpower and physical regime over many months was he able to shake off the effects of the narcotic.

Then were all of the remedies sold at medicine shows blatant frauds and potentially harmful? Frauds, many of them were, because their makers claimed more for them than they could do. Some were harmful—catarrh powders that contained cocaine, tonics so strong in alcohol they masked symptoms in people desperately ill. But the medicine show doctor seldom sold medicines that contained dangerous drugs; those patent medicines exposed by Samuel Hopkins Adams usually were sold through the mail by advertisement or off store shelves. Most pitch doctors specialized in concoctions of vegetables or mineral salts. Depending, perhaps, on the amount of alcohol in the mixture, the show medicines ranged from possibly harmful to harmless to helpful. The smart showman didn't want to poison his customers, because he wanted to go back.

"We could always go back," Cliff Mann said. The Kickapoo Indian and Hamlin's Wizard Oil shows could go back. Many a showman made a living selling medicine on a regular circuit that he followed year after year.

Jumbo, a famous circus elephant exhibited by P. T. Barnum in the late 1800s, is an effective advertisement for the laxative Castoria.

The better medicines did work—in a limited fashion. The liniments, salves and tonics were often effective if used simply to massage sore muscles, soothe irritated skin and relieve constipation. Certain proprietary medicines were based on herbs that are used in modern-day medicines. Some pitch doctors bought their wares from reputable drug firms whose remedies worked to the best of pharmaceutical knowledge of the time. And the medicine showman who made his own products usually knew the ingredients to add to achieve at least a laxative effect.

Black-Draught—probably the most popular laxative the South has ever known—was an example of a harmless purgative. It was an ingredient in Doc McDonald's Compound, and perhaps many a showman added a bit of Black-Draught to his concoctions. People were taking Black-Draught in the days of Davy Crockett, and bottles and boxes of Black-Draught still can be found on the shelves of small-town drugstores. Today the label reads: "Active Ingredient, Senna—Especially compounded with other vegetable products as blending agents." Senna is an herb or shrub, the dried leaves of which have a purgative effect. In the 1950s, the label read: "Senna, Rhubarb, Anise, Peppermint, Cinnamon, Clove, Nutmeg and Other Aromatics in sugar syrup."

The remedy was first compounded by a Tennessee frontiersman, Dr. A. O. Simmons, and later manufactured by his son-in-law, J. H. Thedford. After the Civil War, a Union Army veteran, Z. C. Patten, bought the Black-Draught formula and founded his Chattanooga Medicine Company on the laxative (and on a medicine for "Female Relief" called Wine of Cardui). Before long, many a fence and barn carried the yellow-and-black message "Black-Draught for All the Family."

And Black-Draught, liquid, granulated or powdered, became a staple on pantry shelves right along with the beans. The Southern diet of those days was heavily loaded with pork, gravy, corn bread and biscuits, sure to clog the bowels. Resultant constipation must have made a good laxative like Black-Draught a boon to the South.

Many people still hold the notion that they need a spring tonic to ready their bodies for warmer weather. Certainly the old medical idea that the body occasionally needs purging persisted so strongly into the early part of the twentieth century that the farmer and the small-town merchant opened their wallets to buy those purgatives.

Partly, too, the customer traded his coins for medicine show remedies because his *belief* had been engendered. He believed the medicine would help him, and so in some cases it must have. Acting on that principle, some physicians prescribe a placebo, an inert mixture, for certain patients whose physical pains are the result of mental distress or for some other reasons cannot be treated with real medicine. Psychological studies show evidence that the attitudes of the mind affect the disorders of the body. It is possible that a person with a head cold, given a sugar pill but told that it is an antibiotic, will improve *if he believes the pill will heal him.* If the showman's customer didn't have anything drastically wrong with his body, then the tonics and herb cures, as placebos, may have alleviated his aches and the miseries of daily living.

Believing in the medicine's worth, many a customer felt moved to testify to its worth. "People would get up and testify how our medicine cured them," Cliff Mann said.

Testimonials have always been the assurance, the proffered guarantee of the patent-medicine industry. In the 1830s, T. J. Luster, who called himself a U.S. Indian and German Root Doctor, offered to show numerous testimonials to the success of his healing. U.S. congressmen and senators praised Peruna, their testimonials secured by an active ad man. Hadacol's advertising in the 1940s and 1950s carried the praises of hundreds of men, women and children. With pride and confidence, the Kickapoo Medicine Company published in its circulars such testimonials as this one, written by a man in Pepin, Wisconsin: "I am 68 years old and have suffered over 20 years the excruciating pains of rheumatism. Your Indian Oil and Sagwa have entirely removed the rheumatism from my system."

According to Stewart Holbrook in *The Golden Age of Quackery,* Dr. Arthur J. Cramp, a long-time director of the American Medical Association's Bureau of Investigation, said testimonials generally come from those without scientific knowledge of the medicines and are believed by those who are unable to recognize a fallacy in the statements. Adams, in his studies for *Collier's Weekly,* found fraud in testimonials: business firms that prepared and sold sucker lists of persons who were habitual users of patent medicines and who specialized in giving testimony by category of disease—kidney trouble, heart trouble, cancer, tuberculosis.

These women endorsing Peruna would probably have been shocked to know the tonic contained 28% alcohol.

Yet Dr. Cramp said few testimonials were sold for money or faked by patent medicine firms; most testimonials were documentarily genuine and were given in good faith. It seems some people just enjoy giving their testimony, once they believe in a medicine.

And partly—along with successful use of a remedy and with belief in it—partly the farmer opened his wallet and bought the medicine, because the entertainment of the medicine show, the razzle-dazzle in the cornfield, was a medicine, a balm to the spirit. . . .

6
THE ENTERTAINMENT
"They Loved Us in Greenville"

"We were entertainment coming where they didn't see entertainment from one year to the next," said Cliff. "We played in little towns where they didn't have a movie theater. . . ."

In the 1930s when Doc McDonald's Indian Medicine Show was making its back-country circuit, those little towns didn't have television, either, and it was a rare occasion when the family got into the jalopy to drive twenty-five miles to the nearest large town.

Cliff's wife, Allene, remembers Doc McDonald's show coming to the little Texas farming community where she lived as a girl. "We really looked forward to the show," she said. "We'd get all dressed up, and we'd go to the medicine show every night. There wasn't anything else to do."

Entertainment coming . . .

Pioneer Americans well knew their need for entertainment. They worked hard from before dawn until after dusk. In school and church they were taught the sober virtues that a family should practice: industry, sobriety, thrift, practical scientific knowledge and mutual helpfulness. Those virtues were quoted and urged by essayist Thomas Nixon Carver in an agricultural college textbook in the early 1900s, when Carver referred back to pioneer ways. As for entertainment in rural communities, he said, "Choral singing is the highest form of social amusement known to man." Other worthy entertainments, advised Carver, were church suppers, flag raisings and celebrations of Old Settlers' Day and national holidays. All good and wholesome. But pioneer Americans and their descendants wanted something more: music, drama, jokes, the tears and laughter, the stimulation to the imagination that a live show could bring. To provide a stage for those live shows, one of the first buildings erected in flourishing villages on the frontiers was the "Opera House."

In the winter of 1874–75, this is the kind of entertainment the people of the thirty-year-old Mississippi River town of Keokuk, Iowa, received at their Opera House: Professor Lyman rendering the "Closet Scene" from Shakespeare's *Hamlet;* an Italian Opera Troupe; a concert of the Philharmonic Society; a performance of *Humpty Dumpty* for the children, with "between two and three hundred seats already reserved"—and, perhaps most enjoyed of all, four minstrel shows. "Happy Cal Wagner will shake up the dry bones tomorrow evening with his minstrels," the local newspaper advised on December 1, 1874.

The even more isolated Utah pioneers greeted the smallest medicine show with open arms. Uncle Dutchey's new songs and jokes were memorized in Manti and repeated through the long winter. In another Utah town, early settlers recalled "the joy we felt when the news was brought home that the Medicine Man was in town and would give a free entertainment from his wagon, parked in the heart of town." The whole family trooped out to see the show, the women's hair carefully waved, bustles donned and petticoats starched for the occasion. After the fellow amused the crowd with a ventriloquist's dummy on his knee, he announced his medicine, "Only one dollar for the relief of distress of any physical nature!" In the crowd's rush to buy, parents "were forced to pick up the little ones to protect them from being smothered."

Entertainment—whether a simple gawk at the caged skunk of the Skunk Oil Salve peddler in 1875, a dance and a song by a single performer with a banjo, or a full-fledged vaudeville show, it gladdened the heart of the customer.

Music was always an integral part of any medicine show and perhaps the biggest stimulus of the evening's entertainment. Hear that banjo ripple and plink. Listen to that guitar, strummed sweet and slow in the blues, then rattling in fast time as Happy Mann picks the strings with all five fingers. Thrill to Sousa's marches, played by the big brass band, with the tuba going *whoom-pa!* Tap your feet and sway to Scott Joplin's rags, played by the combo on the medicine show stage, with the piccolo perking, the piano prancing, and the tuba going *whoom-pa!* Open your heart—and your purse.

A good slide trombone man, a good drummer, a good fiddler, could always get a job with a medicine show. He'd be expected to double B and O (band and orchestra), do some kind of act and maybe help take down the canvas tent when the week's stay was done. The bigger shows staged a noon parade to ballyhoo the evening's performance. A wagonful of musicians spread music the length of Main Street, or the members of the band marched to the town square and played a noontime concert, to the special delight of jigging boys and yipping dogs.

The most popular form of entertainment for many years was the minstrel show, featuring banjo players who also rattled the *tickitty-tick* bones. The curtain opens, and there is a half circle of seated minstrels, all dressed in spiffy suits with white gloves and spats, all grinning in blackface with white circles around their eyes and mouths. Whether the performers actually were black or white, all were painted in standard blackface with theatrical makeup.

Leavitt's Monster Minstrels pose formally for their photograph at Bath, N.Y., in 1882.

Sometimes the effect was achieved by burning cork from the inside of bottle caps, mixing it with wet ashes and daubing that on the face. "Mr. Bones, Mr. Bones!" calls the straight man in the middle of the line. "Yessuh, Mr. Interlocutor?" answers an end man. And the show is on, with comedy, song and dance.

Even when audiences grew weary of the unfair parody of the black man and the minstrel show grew less popular, the surefire elements of comedy, song and dance were retained in the variety acts that appeared on the medicine show stages.

Along with music, comedy was at the heart of the medicine show entertainment. Out in Greenville and Keokuk and Punkin Center, year after year the folks laughed at their favorite comedy routines in the medicine shows: "Three O'Clock Train," "Pete in the Well," and "Over the River, Charlie." Comedians knew the skits by heart and improvised their variations. Here is one version of "Three O'Clock Train":

> The interior is a wretched set; two chairs and an old banjo are the only props in a bare and dingy room, which appears in half-light and is sinisterly suggestive. The two characters are a straight man and an eccentric comic—long coat, umbrella, absurd little hat and fright wig. The straight man is seated, and the comic enters.

COMIC: What time does the three o'clock train go out?
STRAIGHT: The three o'clock train? Why, it goes out exactly sixty minutes past two o'clock.
COMIC: That's funny. The man at the station told me it went out exactly sixty minutes before four o'clock.
STRAIGHT: Well, you won't miss your train, anyway.
COMIC (*seating himself*): Nice place you have here.
STRAIGHT: I get this house rent-free, because it is haunted.
COMIC (*looking around nervously*): I'm not afraid of ghosts. My

grandmother used to keep a ghost boardinghouse. Some of my best friends are ghosts.

STRAIGHT: Well, I'm glad to hear that, because this house is full of ghosts.

COMIC: When do the, that is, when, er, where are they, these, er . . . ?

STRAIGHT: Oh, they're liable to come in anytime.

COMIC (*shuddering*): Right in here?

STRAIGHT: Oh yes, right in here. They just waft in and waft right out again.

COMIC: They, they waft, do they? (*looks around uneasily*)

STRAIGHT: What's the matter?

COMIC: I thought something was wafting.

STRAIGHT (*singing a "lively" song to cheer up Comic; in a dismal wail he begins*):

> *The old jaw bone on the almshouse wall . . .*

As Straight sings, the stage lights dim, and weird sounds are heard from backstage. Comic shivers in terror but insists he's not afraid, as Straight embarks on the second verse:

> *At twelve o'clock near the hour of one,*
> *A figure appears that will strike you dumb.*
> *He grabs you by the hair of the head,*
> *And he grabs you about until you are dead.*

Offstage noises and wails. Straight Man rises and Ghost enters, and Straight Man exits, singing:

> *Oh, the old jaw bone, the old jaw bone . . .*

COMIC (*still unaware of the Ghost*): Why not sing something we both know? We'll sing it together. Yours is a good song, but I don't know the way it ends. (*Ghost nudges Comic.*)

COMIC: I wasn't asleep. I was just listening to the music. Is it most time for them ghosts to waft?

Comic looks casually to one side and sees part of white sheet. He follows his glance, takes in Ghost completely and rises, horrified, as Ghost rises with him. He pulls the string of his fright wig, and hair stands straight up. Recovering somewhat, Comic edges away and then dashes around stage, and Ghost, his finger pointing at Comic, pursues. As Ghost gradually gains on Comic, Comic exits, diving through breakaway window.

CURTAIN

Variations of the comic ghost show were enjoyed all over the country. In 1930 a man named F. J. Clifford recalled the medicine show that came to his town every year when he was a child, and his favorite part of the entertainment was the "ghost scene." Each year he and the other children rushed to the FREE medicine show and sat with drowsy eyes through the pitch doctor's lecture until someone nudged, "Hey, wake up, you're gonna miss the ghost scene!" There on the stage is a man painted in blackface, seated beside a rough facsimile of a tombstone. He has been hired to spend a night in the graveyard, the man announces, and he isn't afraid of ghosts. He has a song to ward off the spirits: "Oh, the old jawbone . . ."

A ghost rises up behind him and places a hand on the man's shoulder. Not a sound from the children, thrilled silent with the terror of it all. Wide-eyed, they watch as the man tries to slide away from the ghost and at last flees offstage. Leaning forward in excitement, the children wait for the *thud-thud* of feet, when the man and the ghost burst across the stage again.

Clifford added he couldn't remember how the ghost scene ended, only that it was the most wonderful show he had ever seen.

Mae Noell, who, like Cliff Mann, traveled with her family's medicine show in the 1920s, remembers with delight the nonsense songs her father used to warm up the audiences. Between verses, while the crowd laughed, he would sing "Deedle dee dee" until the people were ready for the next verse:

There sits a fellow, 'way back there
In the fifth row and in the third chair.
Pants is rolled up so his socks can be seen,
I'll betcha five dollars that his feet ain't clean.
CHORUS
That's what the old black crow told me,
In a hick-o-ry tree, dee dee deedle dee dee dee
REPEAT
Dee-dee dee deedle dee dee dee.
VERSE 2
There stands a couple right over there,
Ain't gonna tell ya jest ezackly where.
Betcha five dollars that the girl don't know
The boy borrowed money to buy candy at the show!

In the twentieth century, the medicine show increasingly became a traveling vaudeville show. Many an actor, musician, dancer and magician found steady work with a medicine show for a season. Besides the band, there were the strong-man acts, the standard comedy routines, the fire-eaters, the acrobats, the solo musical acts, the balloon ascensions—and parachute drops. *Billboard*, the show-business paper, helped the pitch doctor and his performers to get together. In the 1920s a typical classified ad in *Billboard* read:

Motorized show wants dramatic people for medicine company. General business team doing specialties. Actor musicians, novelty act. Make salary low. You get it. Best of accommodations and cook house. We carry workingmen, but all male members must assist on moving days. Be truthful. State all in first.

In his book *Medicine Show*, Malcolm Webber told just how much a performer was expected to do when he joined up with a medicine showman. When Webber was in his late teens, he hired on with the Ton-Ko-Ko Medicine Show as a drummer. Soon he learned that in order to hold his position he had to do "bits in acts."

Showman William P. Burt and the troupe of a liniment show. The pitch doctor is seated in the center, and Burt is seated at his left.

Some of the musicians solved that problem by working up a simple song-and-dance routine, and often they teamed with a girl in the company, so that they had a double act, too. The dance routine might be a rattling clog on a metal plate or the old soft-shoe on sand, the soft-soled shoes without metal taps making a rhythmic whispering on the sand. Three musicians might become strolling Italian minstrels singing "Santa Lucia." Or they'd work up a musical novelty such as a jug band. One act, that must have been a horror, was a double quartet of Jew's harps.

Webber praised a performer named Jack Clough as the most versatile of them all. Not only did Clough play tuba in the band and bass viol in the orchestra, but he could fill in on piano, mandolin, banjo and guitar. For "bits," Clough did comedy skits in blackface; he was a good hoofer at buck-and-wing, clog and soft-shoe dancing; as a song stylist he talked his songs; he did a tumbling act that included an effortless double somersault; and his triumph was a sleight-of-hand act in which he manipulated cards and coins. Clough also helped manage the Ton-Ko-Ko show.

Since a vaudeville turn was necessary, Webber practiced to be a strong man, or "iron worker." He bent iron spikes in his hands or his teeth, he broke rocks with his fist, he pulled horses with his hair and, before long, Webber was billed as "Atlas, Man of Muscle." Most of the strong-man acts were tricks, Webber said. For instance, when bending a spike, he would wrap the spike in a towel, "to protect my hands," then produce a prebent spike from the towel. Rock breaking was a matter of selecting "soft" rocks.

Webber's strong-hair act was on the level, though. In a town square on market day, he would pull a team of horses or a loaded wagon around the square. To do that, he twisted a large metal comb in his hair, attached one end of a rope to the comb and the other end to the wagon—and *pulled.* Pulling the horses was harder, he said. The rope from his hair was fastened to one team of horses, while Webber looped around his elbows another rope to a second team of horses Then the two teams were urged to strain in opposite directions, and Webber's feat was to hold them in place by his hair and his arms. Webber didn't explain how he developed such a strong attachment of his hair to his scalp.

Strong-man acts were always popular with the country crowds in the earlier days. One time Cliff Mann announced for a strong man down in Texas.

"One of his gigs was, he'd drive a car around town while he was blindfolded," Cliff told. "There was a trick to that—glycerine in the makeup in his eyebrows, which helped him to see. As the blindfold was being tied on, he'd squeeze his eyes shut tight, bringing his eyebrows down. The glycerine would stick to the cloth, and when he opened his eyes and raised his eyebrows, the blindfold would pull up just enough so he could see out from under it. There wasn't any trick to his strong jaws, though. Pick up people in chairs. . . . Why, he'd pull two or three cars hooked to a silk sash between his teeth, bracing himself against buildings and pulling those cars down the street. He had the strongest jaws of anybody I saw in my life."

Some performers made lifelong careers of entertaining in medicine shows. Some were Broadway actors or musicians temporarily "at liberty," who picked up eating money with a tour in "the sticks." Still others, like Webber, were youngsters who joined a show somewhere along the road and either had a short fling at show biz or worked up through the medicine shows to fame on the Broadway stages or in the movies.

Quite a few of the actors and comedians famous in the 1920s, such as Hal Skelly and the Weaver Brothers, started their careers passing out medicine from a show-wagon tailgate. In 1950 and 1951, when Senator LeBlanc's big Hadacol show first toured the South and then played a month's stand in Los Angeles, LeBlanc featured top performers. Name entertainers who lent their talents to the Hadacol medicine shows included Judy Garland, Groucho Marx,

Chico Marx, Minnie Pearl, Cesar Romero, Mickey Rooney, Roy Acuff, Carmen Miranda, Connie Boswell, George Burns and Gracie Allen.

Even poets took a turn as medicine show minstrels. In the nineteenth century both Eugene Field and James Whitcomb Riley traveled with medicine shows in their youth.

One summer day in 1872, Dr. S. B. McCrillus drove into Riley's hometown, Greenfield, Indiana, to sell his Standard Remedies—Oriental Ointment, European Balsam, and so on. When the medicine showman moved on, young Riley went with him as "graphic advertising agent"—sign painter. They traveled in a springboard wagon filled with buffalo robes and medicine bottles. Soon Riley was decorating barns, bridges and fences with the message "Go to Ward's Drug Store for McCrillus' Popular Standard Remedies."

James Riley returned home for the winter, but the taste for life on the road stayed with him. In 1875, when he saw Doc C. M. Townsend rolling down Greenfield's streets in a covered wagon, Riley signed on with Townsend's unit of the Hamlin's Wizard Oil shows. This time Riley doubled and expanded his talents. Not only did he paint signs, but he worked up a chalk-talk act with such medical illustrations as a bottle of Townsend's Cholera Balm on legs, with a smile on the cork, warding off a skeleton labeled Death. Riley beat the drum in Townsend's band and also played violin solos. In the evening's entertainment he sang, recited poems of his own and improvised comic songs and ballads.

Years later, Riley said, "The ballads came from incidents on the road. They were written on dull, hot Sundays in selfish country towns where the church bells barked at strangers while lazy men rolled round in narrow bits of shade."

In memory of Dr. McCrillus, Riley wrote:

> *Wherever blooms of health are blown,*
> *McCrillus' Remedies are known.*

> *His Oriental Liniment*
> *Is known to fame to such extent*
> *That orders for it emanate*
> *From every portion of the state;*
> *His European Balsam, too,*
> *Sends blessings down to me and you.*

Dramatic and musical acts were not the only medicine show entertainment that made the customers sit up in their seats or stand on tiptoe to see over the crowd. The contests and "giveaways" were part of the evening's excitement. Doc McDonald's show featured the diamond-ring contest. At the Ton-Ko-Ko show it was the "popular lady" contest, in which each purchase of a bottle of herb medicine constituted a vote for the customer's favorite lady. Ton-Ko-Ko's prize for the most popular lady was a silver tea or coffee service.

Whether it was an imitation gold watchcase, Vital Sparks or a bottle of cheap perfume, the sucker always jumped up to get something for nothing. Clifford, of the ghost-scene memories, said the pitch doctor spurred lagging sales by offering free finger rings and gold watch chains. People thronged forward to receive. Clifford told how his Uncle Rufus, a tall old Scotsman, stretched his arms over everybody to clutch a massive gold watch chain, "his lower jaw rising and falling in nervous eagerness."

But of all the forms of entertainment, the medicine showman himself probably was the most entrancing. Jude McDonald was "the man the crowd had been waiting for, because he never showed himself until then." And Doc McDonald, Doc Jim Lighthall, Princess Lotus Blossom, all gave the people their money's worth in dramatic performance. Sometimes the pitch doctor even rigged his act as the only entertainment, and it was sufficient to hold the crowd and sell the medicine.

Arthur Hammer was a famous muscle reader. In order to pitch medicine he ballyhooed with "The Australian Murder Mystery," which he proceeded to solve blindfolded. The act went like this: Hammer would tie a blindfold over his eyes and ask that a pocketknife be given to one of the spectators. That person was to pretend to stab another man and then hide the knife in the clothing of a third person. Hammer announced he would identify the murderer, the victim and the very knife. All he needed was a volunteer to guide him through the crowd.

Immediately some onlooker became part of the act, and Hammer, who truly could not see, exercised his great skill as a muscle reader. With the man's hand on his wrist, Hammer wove rapidly through the standing audience, and no matter how honest the man might be in not giving signals, his muscles twitched involuntarily when he and Hammer came close to the murderer, the victim and the holder of the knife. With practiced attention, Hammer could interpret the slightest muscle movement and change in the grip on his wrist.

To vary his act, Arthur Hammer, blindfolded, drove a buggy through town on a route selected by a committee but not divulged to Hammer. He vowed he would turn every corner of the preplanned route. If he could do it, in return he would be allowed to sell medicine in that town without a license. Someone was chosen to hold Hammer's wrist, and off they rolled in the buggy, Hammer holding the reins. He always shouted the horses to a fast trot, to his passenger's dismay, because "the faster we drive, the more muscle signals he gives me!" Hammer seldom had to pay the license fee. Even if some townspeople were onto Hammer's act, it must have been worth the price of a license to watch the exercise of such an exotic skill.

But watching a medicine showman go through his pitch and skillfully work his con may have been the best entertainment of all for many a customer, even if he didn't believe all of the pitch doctor's brash claims. Several people have written down their memories of the medicine showmen who came to their towns, and their accounts say it was a pleasure to watch the men work with their wits. Recently a retired Army colonel named Mike told a tale that illustrates the point.

Mike had met a young con artist named Bumps when both were buck privates at the beginning of World War II. One Saturday afternoon at a camp in Texas, Bumps said, "Let's go to town." Mike replied that he was down to fifteen cents. "That's plenty," said Bumps.

The two privates hitched a ride to town, and Bumps led the way to a drugstore, where he bought a big bar of castile soap for a nickel. He proceeded to cut the bar of soap into sixteen small squares and wrapped them in tissue paper from his pocket. The remaining dime was invested in two nickel beers at a tavern that Bumps selected because the bartender was wearing glasses. In the back was a kitchen, where the bartender also did the cooking for light snacks.

"Must be hard on you to cook wearing glasses," Bumps said. "I'll bet your glasses steam up."

"Oh, yes," the man agreed.

Bumps then told a tale of a friend who had invented an antifogging material, but the "rich guys" wouldn't let him patent it, so the friend was peddling it privately. Bumps just happened to have a small sample in his pocket. Want to try? Of course. Bumps rubbed a little chunk of soap over the man's glasses, then huffed his breath on the glass.

"See, the glass doesn't fog up!"

Of course, the soap had left ever so slight a coating on the glasses, so steam didn't affect them.

Bumps sold that chunk of soap to the delighted bartender for fifty cents. Mike and Bumps moved on to other cafés and taverns, touting the "antifogging material" to cooks and bartenders wearing glasses, until all the bits of soap had been sold, and the privates had eight dollars to spend on their evening's entertainment. The most amusement, though, as Mike remembers it now, was in watching Bumps work it.

Even those of us without an inch of larceny in our souls grin at such a display. Why do we laugh, when we know very well that pitch doctor is conning us?

"I guess we admire someone who can live by his wits," Mike said.

After all, we figure with the pioneer, the farmer, the small-town merchant, even if the medicine doesn't work, it only cost a quarter or a dollar. The important thing is, the pitch doctor has put on a good show. Not only have his performers provided us with entertainment in music, comedy and dance, but the medicine showman has given us a fascinating display of a con man making his pitch, a virtuoso performance of a man working with his wits. The artist is worthy of his hire.

7
COUNTING UP THE RECEIPTS
Why Did They Do It?

Why did they do it? Why would so many medicine showmen try to con so many people out of their paltry quarters and dollars?

But wait a minute! Those fellows were selling *medicine.* Their publicly stated purpose was philanthropy: "I bring you this medicine to cure your ails." Didn't any pitch doctor enter the medicine show business, as a young man or woman enters the medical profession, in order to help sick people? It is possible that some of the concocters of proprietary brews did want to offer a good medicine, and it is probable that some of the tonics and liniments did relieve constipation and rheumatic pains. But the most that any of the showmen claimed privately was: "Our medicine wouldn't hurt you. It might have helped some."

Why did they do it? Well, for money, to start with, for profit. The Diamond King counted up his take behind the closed tent flap near Alamo Plaza. After the show, Brother Jonathan bent over a cheap notebook at an improvised desk to add up the evening's sizable receipts. Those quarters and dollars could add up, and the pitch doctor always hoped for the big strike.

Violet, Princess Lotus Blossom, sent telegrams to her friends the first time her street pitches took in $100 in one day. The profits from the Kickapoo Indian Medicine Company brought fortunes to partners John Healy and Charles Bigelow. They built mansions in New Haven, Connecticut, and lived handsomely for the thirty-year run of the Kickapoo shows. When the partners sold the business in 1912, it is said they received a total of $250,000. Jim Ferdon, the Quaker showman, made a fortune and kept it.

When they were in the money, medicine men lived high. Restaurant owners always were glad to see the pitch doctor and his wife coming, because they ordered champagne by the case for their friends and spread around generous tips. Violet described the rich dress of the clan of medicine showmen and their women in the early part of the century; full dress suits, top hats and fancy canes for the men; elaborate evening dresses, ostrich plumes, sealskin jackets and diamond sunbursts for the women. 1880 to 1910—those were the most prosperous, high-riding times for the hucksters in the huge medicine show business.

But Doc Jim Lighthall, Indian scout of the magnetic personality, is believed to have died a pauper in Texas. A certain Diamond Dick was still wearing diamond buttons on his coat and vest when he was killed in a gunfight in Oklahoma, but he had not a dollar in his pockets.

Violet McNeal told that she lost her diamonds, her bank account, her beauty, her health and nearly her life when she became heavily addicted to drugs through her medicine show contacts. Her pitchman husband had introduced her to smoking opium while she was still in her teens. Later, after she had undergone desperate withdrawal from drugs and had recovered, Violet made a modest living as Madame V. Pasteur, wearing an academic gown and selling her herb medicines.

Why then would a pitch doctor keep pitching medicine for a bare living?

"My dad could have stayed put and made a real living as a boot and harness maker," Cliff Mann said. "But you couldn't chain him in one place. He and Jude had too much talent to stay in one place and do honest hard work. It was always *Move on, Hit the road!*" If the show ran out of money, Jude would sometimes go to work as a carpenter. When times were especially hard, he and Happy Mann cut out scrub oak sprouts from farmers' fields at fifty cents an acre. But that kind of work was done only to get a road stake—traveling money.

The medicine show business seemed to attract men and women who enjoyed the adventurous life on the road, always traveling on to new places, new people, new chances for big medicine sales. Like a gambler, the pitch doctor was ready to take chances; it was an exciting gamble that he could persuade people to buy his medicine.

"I'm Electric Bill from over the hill; never worked and never will!" sang Jim Ferdon, when he was starting out. Big Foot Bill Wallace, who sold a gee-whizz purple satin "electric" belt treated with vinegar on zinc, sang the same song: "I'm Big Foot Bill from over the hill; I never worked, and I never will."

Charles Mundell of the Market Street medicine store wrote: "I have never willingly done a day's work in my life. . . . I have always been a little too light for heavy work, and a little too heavy for light work, so all I've ever done without compulsion—is talk!"

And yet, for a man who didn't like work, the pitch doctor certainly used a lot of energy up there on that stage, hustling his wares. Maybe that was the point. He was up there on that stage.

"You see, Uncle Jude was a ham, just plain ham. During the day all he lived for was performing in the show that night. Up on that stage he was in a world of his own. He talked long and high-pressure. . . . He had a talent for selling. . . ."

They were talkers, all. Medicine men prided themselves on their gift of gab. They polished it, exploited it, gloried in it. Nothing made a pitch doctor happier than to hold and sway an audience with his voice, playing out his line, snagging the crowd, pulling it

A medicine man draws a crowd at a county fair, about 1910.

in with finesse. It was talk used for a purpose; the medicine showman delighted in the skillful way he worked his con.

Curly Thurber, a labor union agitator, was a pitch doctor who seemed to love to play with words, as much to amuse himself as to amaze the crowd. One time when he was spieling to an audience of migrant workers and vagrants on Burnside Street in Portland, Oregon, Curly said, "If you go to those high-powered doctors, you know what they'll do to you? They'll cut open your umbilicus and yank out your tweedium!" The skid-row crowd leaped forward to buy Curly's medicine and avoid that awful fate.

Charles Mundell said expansively, "I like to talk. To lecture. To preach. I am never happy unless I am either talking or writing. When my throat gets too sore to talk, I write. Either serves to gratify my inordinate craving to be heard."

Mundell said that he started his preaching life as a boy evangelist and became an ordained minister of the Baptist church. When he fell away from the church, he said, he still had to preach something to people, so he switched to proclaiming "the curative value of our Indian Herbs for the ills of their bodies!"

It was in church, too, that Violet McNeal first moved people with her voice. At revival meetings in her girlhood she was always asked to sing "Come Unto Me," and she recalled the thrill of power she felt when people came weeping to the altar while she sang.

Brother Jonathan's rich voice crooned as he played on his audience, outrageously yet subtly associating himself and his Giver of Life medicine with the Healer, Jesus Christ.

To many an unsophisticated person in the audience, the medicine show doctor was some kind of superior being. The potential customer regarded the powerful, flamboyant pitch doctor with a mixture of awe, amusement and hero worship. The medicine man knew it and loved it. He took pride in the admiration of a crowd, and he took purchases of medicine as testimony to his power to con.

Many a medicine man did indeed feel superior to those he had been able to con. Privately he called his customer yokel, sucker, simp, hick, scissor-bill, rube, gill, native, chump. A *squawker* was a complaining customer. A *tip* was a small crowd; a large crowd was a *push*.

Talking about handling people, Violet said the audience "is easy to dominate, if you are sure of yourself." If the pitch doctor spoke with authority, the audience would follow like a bunch of sheep, she declared.

The showman's terms for his medicines were tinged with cynicism as well. Any salve was called *grease*; liquid medicine was *slum*; herbs were *chopped grass*, and powdered herbs were *flea powder*. In the medicine show slang, *slum* might also refer to any cheap merchandise. *Cornpunk* was any salve for corns on the toes. A gaudy display of merchandise or of the showman's costume was *flash*. His expenses were the *nut*, and profits were *velvet*.

And there was the *reader*, the license the pitchman had to buy to sell medicine in a town. In the early part of the twentieth century, many towns began to charge any traveling peddler with a license fee.

After the Pure Food and Drug Act went into effect in 1907, and magazine articles began to acquaint more and more people with the frauds in quack medicines, many towns were closed to the traveling medicine show. If the town was open, the license fee for doing business there grew higher and higher. By the 1920s, a county license fee in some parts of the South could run as high as $1000.

Medicine shows also encountered increased hostility from town officials, who were suspicious of any con artist. True, there were the medicine showmen who held fairly ethical standards and sold fairly reliable medicines. The Kickapoo company enjoyed such a good reputation that showmen begged the owners for contracts to sell the Indian remedies in specific territories. When they granted those rights, Healy and Bigelow imposed strict regulations on shows bearing the Kickapoo name. The Hamlin's Wizard Oil merchants too achieved an air of respectability; they were welcomed back to towns year after year; local storekeepers were glad to stock the Hamlin medicines. After all, people needed to buy cough syrups and laxatives somewhere, and certain of those sold at medicine shows were effective and harmless.

But some of the smaller shows traveling the towns sold medicine that made people sick; the awkward performers failed to entertain; the con was too obvious. Sometimes those shows had to leave town hurriedly in the night to avoid arrest or a posse of irate citizens bearing equipment for tarring and feathering the medicine showman. The reputation of the Kickapoo company and its Sagwa medicine was hurt by unauthorized imitators who sold rotten concoctions under similar names, such as Awaga, and whose Indian shows were scruffy. Worst were the pitch doctors who fleeced the people shamelessly. They featured private consultations in their temporary offices, offered to cure major ailments for large fees and sometimes managed to acquire the client's life's savings.

In his old age in the late 1920s, Nevada Ned Oliver recounted the rising trouble with thoroughly dishonest men within the pitch business. He called them "jamb workers," "jamb" being any form of illegitimate selling. Some of the traveling pitchmen who soured town after town did not sell medicine but promoted other items. For example, there were the Give Back operators, who worked with small bulk items, such as jewelry or fake gold watchcases. Spieling from a buggy or the back of a light wagon, the operator attracted an audience by offering to give away his wares. For advertising purposes, he said, his company wished to place its new product in that town. All he asked was that a customer put up some money to show his good faith.

Following a formula, the pitchman talked rapidly, "The money is mine? I can keep it, donate it to charity, or give it back? Very well, now I will show you my good faith." He gave back the quarters and allowed the people to keep their free imitation cameo brooches and, next, gold-washed pins. Any doubts of suspicious persons were quieted.

Then came the gimmick, the "gold" watchcase, which easily was worth ten dollars at any jewelry store, he said. Who would put up five dollars, just to show good faith? Hands thrust forward eagerly, and the operator gathered in the five-dollar bills. "I can keep the money, throw it away, or give it back?" he repeated the formula. "Very well, then, folks, I'll keep it." He whipped up his horse, which trotted away before the crowd could gather its wits. And the crowd seldom gave chase, because each man was convinced his "gold" watchcase was worth more than the five dollars he had paid, anyway. Later, when the victims realized the cases were made of brass or stamped tin, the Give Back operator was long gone.

The worst kind of jamb worker was the casetaker, the consulting doctor, Ned Oliver said. The show was operated as a blind or come-on for consultations afterward in an office with the doctor. To satisfy the law, he was a graduate physician with a medical license. He might be an alcoholic has-been or a competent doctor; it didn't matter. His business in the office was to relieve the customer of as much money as he could. The ailment always could be cured by the show's particular brand of medicine or the doctor's gimmick. Violet told of a casetaker who called himself an "iridologist" and who offered, in exchange for a large fee, to diagnose all bodily conditions by looking at the customer's eyes.

In indignation Oliver said he'd seen a woman dying of dropsy persuaded to mortgage her home to pay for worthless treatment. Oliver had known of phony consulting offices that took in as much as $1000 a day.

The legitimate medicine showmen grew to hate the jamb workers for the "trail of closed towns, exorbitant licenses and public suspicion" they left behind them. In defense against the nefarious practices of jamb workers, the singularly individualistic pitch doctors banded together and formed the National Pitchmen's and Salesmen's Protective Association. The pitchmen held their first convention for mutual cooperation in Cincinnati in 1927. Only those with a legitimate product to sell were welcome.

The medicine showman regarded himself not as a lowdown thief but as a colorful entrepreneur. He gave the customers a good show and acceptable medicine—he gave them their money's worth. That image must have been important to him. William Burt, whose vocal quartet once traveled with a liniment show, told what happened when the Doctor lost his self-image.

An honored physician and surgeon, the Doctor had suffered a nervous breakdown and had turned to the medicine show business to make a living while regaining his mental health. He discovered a talent for speaking. His powerful lectures and demonstrations were so effective that liniment sales flourished, and customers were grateful. The liniment really did seem to relieve rheumatism temporarily, and soon the Doctor was taking away crutches from the crippled, who walked off the stage rejoicing, after he'd rubbed them vigorously with his compound.

Unfortunately, one customer was dissatisfied when his pain returned, and he came back after the Doctor with a gun that night. Forewarned, the Doctor dismissed the vocal quartet and tried to get out of town at once. No train was leaving soon, so he set out on foot. In the dark he heard dogs baying behind him and pictured a lynching posse with bloodhounds chasing him, led by the man with the gun. The frightened Doctor scrambled up a tree to hide—and saw a rabbit run under the tree, chased by a couple of barking dogs.

When he rejoined the quartet two days later in another town, the Doctor told the tale on himself with humorous detail and extravagant gesture. Yet the incident seemed to have destroyed his carefully built-up image of himself. From that time, Burt said, the Doctor's lectures became feeble and stammering, his powers of salesmanship declined, liniment sales dropped, and the show folded in Joplin, Missouri.

Occasionally a pitchman must have had misgivings about his way of life. One man wrote of the night he had a flat tire and went to a farmhouse for aid. After he'd been given a generous supper and had sat on the porch in the dusk with the farmer, listening to the crickets chirp, he wondered, "Is the game really worth the candle?" The farmer had "a nice home, staunch friends and the love of a good woman," while the medicine man had to move on with his racket. "Which one of us is the chump?"

Nevertheless, it was *Move on, Hit the road!* Why did they do it?

Some pitch doctors took pride in conning the customers: "They'll follow you like sheep," said Violet. Others took pleasure in satisfying the customers: "Those good old farmers sure were glad to see our show coming!" said Cliff.

"To go unnoticed was the ultimate insult," said Nevada Ned, and there's the key. Most important, the medicine man was the focal point of attention, the powerful center of the show. Many a farm boy like Charlie Bigelow or Jim Ferdon must have looked at a medicine show doctor and said to himself, "I want to be somebody wonderful like him!"

"Up on that stage Uncle Jude was in a world of his own...." Never mind that Indian Jude had come along thirty years too late to cash in on the Indian medicine craze. Up on that stage ... he flourished his talent for talking, his talent for selling, his love of conning. Doc Jude McDonald and all the pitch doctors in whose tradition he followed were that ego-satisfying mixture of ham actor, cunning manipulator and play-acting child dressed in dramatic costume. Up on that stage he was a Very Important Person.

The medicine man conned himself into believing it, and that, his biggest con of all, may have been his most precious reward from the medicine show business.

AFTERWORD

The traveling medicine show made its last rounds through the rural areas of the U.S. in the 1940s, and it was dead by the mid-1950s.

Yet daily we can see and hear modern versions of the medicine show on television and radio. Entertainment interests the customer, then is interrupted by dramatic commercials making the pitch for the medicine. The pitch doctor is now the actor who claims "instant relief," who declares, "Nine out of ten doctors prescribe . . . ." Patent medicines of today are the pain relievers and sleeping pills, deodorants and foot powders, cough syrups and cold cures, so widely advertised. We still have the standard medicine show wares: preparations for relief of upset stomachs, liniments for sore muscles, salves for minor cuts and abrasions. And of course, we still have the purgatives for relief of constipation—the old "physic show" set to radio and television.

But nowadays the compounds of pain relievers generally are based on aspirin rather than on the opium of nineteenth-century painkillers. Instead of alcohol in tonics, we have vitamins to supplement our health needs. Also, as of 1962, we have a federal law that requires drug manufacturers to prove that a medicine actually works as claimed, as well as being safe to use.

Progress has been made in customer protection—yet some advertisers still use the word "miracle" in their claims about medicines. MIRACLE DIET PILLS, a newspaper ad proclaims in large type, then goes on to say that it's no miracle but a fact that the pills curb the appetite, and so persons taking the pills will lose weight. The law requires that those pills work as claimed, but it seems it is still permissible to hint at a miracle cure. The customer needs to read or listen carefully to sort out the facts in an advertisement. Samuel Hopkins Adams, the reporter who crusaded in 1905 for the first pure food and drug law, was demanding in 1958 that the claims made in advertising be identical with the claims on the product's label. At present no law requires that, according to the Federal Trade Commission, which has authority over advertising claims. In 1972 the Federal Drug Administration began a review of the safety and efficacy of all over-the-counter drugs, as patent medicines have come to be called. When the study is completed, an FTC spokesman said, "Specific regulations as to efficacy claims and directions for use in labeling will be in effect for every over-the-counter drug."

Effects of the FDA survey, FTC enforcement and self-policing of the advertising industry can already be seen. For example, a recent ruling specifies that Listerine mouthwash can no longer claim to prevent colds. In the past few years, most television medicine commercials admonish the viewer to "take only as directed."

However, the same old pitch about "nature's remedies" and "the natural way" to health and beauty continues to lure customers to buy obscure health foods, herb medicines and cosmetics possibly based on some newly discovered wonder vegetable from the Middle East. In 1843 an advertising specialist declared that pain and the

The order in which over-the-counter drugs will be evaluated by the FDA.

The FDA plans to evaluate 25 categories of over-the-counter drugs. The following listing indicates the order in which the Agency intends to call for data from the industry. As the Review Program develops, some realignments and/or redefinitions may become necessary. The Requests for Data and Information will be printed in the *Federal Register*. Sixty days will be allowed for submission.

1. Antacids
2. Antimicrobials
3. Sedatives & sleep aids
4. Analgesics
5. Cold remedies & antitussives
6. Antihistamines
7. Mouthwashes
8. Anti-infectives
9. Antirheumatics
10. Hematinics
11. Vitamins-minerals
12. Antiperspirants
13. Laxatives
14. Dentifrices & dental products
15. Sunburn treatments & preventives
16. Contraceptives
17. Stimulants
18. Hemorrhoidals
19. Antidiarrheals
20. Dandruff preparations
21. Bronchodilators & antiasthmatics
22. Antiemetics
23. Ophthalmics
24. Menstrual products
25. Emetics

In 1972, the Federal Drug Administration began a lengthy review of this list of over-the-counter drugs. So far, reports have been given on several categories, including antacids and sedatives.

fear of pain generates the strongest attention in mankind, with personal vanity running second in appeal. Modern advertisers of medicines and cosmetics know the market is still there.

When asked, Could the traveling medicine show make a comeback? Cliff Mann said:

> No, medicine shows wouldn't go today, because the entertainment couldn't draw. Nowadays people can get all the entertainment they want on television, where there is high-priced talent that a traveling medicine show couldn't command. Oh yes, people might go to look at a med show once, out of nostalgia or novelty. But I doubt the show could keep going back, like we did in the old days.
>
> There was a time when people wanted to see us show people in their little towns, but then the movies knocked us out of business. Those old farmers, they got to going to see the movies instead of coming to see us. Well, I figured we might as well get in on the money, adapt movies to the medicine show. We could bring movies to those people, if that was what they'd rather see.
>
> In 1936, the last summer I traveled with my family's outfit, I talked Uncle Jude into building me a little projection room on a two-wheeled trailer. He bought me a sixteen-millimeter projector, some film and a big sheet. We took our traveling movies and our medicine down to those little towns in south Texas that still didn't have a movie theater, and we flashed films on the sheet in a tent.
>
> At first we just showed the movies between our regular shows, but the movies got to be more popular than the live entertainment. Which didn't make Jude and my dad and the actors too happy. But I had those movies tuned to the kind of town we were in. If we were in a real religious Southern Baptist town, then they'd get religious shows; if we were down where there were Mexicans, they'd see a Mexican show; and of course, there were the old cowboy movies. Those south Texas people loved it. But

showing tent movies wasn't what you'd call a big money-maker.

Those days, 1937, 1938, the money was in the movie theaters, and I decided to go where the business was. When I got out of high school in 1937, I didn't go back with the family show. Instead I headed down into Texas, and in one little town, in order to get some coin, I moved a piece of furniture for a man who ran the local movie theater. Then I asked the man for a job.

I said, "I can do anything you can do, and I can whip anybody that works for you. I want to be a showman."

So the man liked that, and he hired me. I went to work for five dollars a week selling popcorn and cleaning up the theater after the show. But the best thing, at the end of the first week the man took me out of those overalls I had worn all my life. He bought me a pair of pants, those salt-and-pepper pants that flared at the bottom. And a pair of two-tone black-and-white shoes. Whoo-ee, I was something else! I was on my way! I moved up to ticket boy, then operating the projector, then painting the advertisements—the big boards out in front, with the cutout heads, banners, posters and so on. I worked there up until World War II, when I went into the Navy.

After I got out of the service I went back to show business, managing movie theaters. And the advertising methods and gimmicks that I had learned with the medicine shows went right to work advertising movies. There must have been plenty of us raised in medicine shows who contributed a lot to theater business.

People's curiosity! How we could use that! I remembered how Dad would attract a crowd for one of his sidewalk demonstrations. He'd get out there on a street corner with a yardstick, and he'd look up at the sky, and then he'd hold out the yardstick, like he's measuring something in the sky, and he'd write down some figures. Look up, study the yardstick, write figures, over and over, until he had about fifteen or twenty people stopped, looking up, watching him, wondering what the heck he was measuring. And then he'd go into his corn salve demonstration.

Well, one time for a movie come-on I used people's curiosity that way. Out in front of the theater I put a barrel all duded up with chains around it and big locks on the chains, and there was a sign, said "Beware! Only two spotted bats in southern New Mexico. Very dangerous in flight!" Of course, we had a convenient hole in the top of the barrel. People would stop and look in that hole, every one of them. They'd even stop their cars and get out to look. What they'd see in the bottom of the barrel was two brickbats spotted with white paint. And they'd laugh and shake their heads, but they'd notice the movie.

Another gimmick was, I'd paint over a window with white calcimine in some vacant building and leave one peephole in the paint, fairly high up. On the window I'd put a sign that read, "If you are not tall enough to see through this hole, please do not stand on a box." I'd leave a handy box nearby. And every single person that went by would get up on that box and look. They couldn't resist it! What they'd see through the peephole was a sign inside announcing a coming movie.

I still had the traveling blood in me, so over the next twenty-five years I managed movie theaters in Texas, New Mexico, Oregon and Colorado. I met my wife in a theater in West Texas, where I was running the projector and Allene was running the candy-and-popcorn stand. My daughter, Jodi, grew up in those little apartments behind the movie-projector booths, did her homework in a back row of the theater, eating popcorn.

I was proud of show business in those days, but I'm not anymore. The pornography, it's not show business, it's a racket! Look at the movie listings for the month in this *Boxoffice* magazine. Look at that stuff. I couldn't book enough decent shows to keep a movie house open for a month. That's why I finally quit, back in 1963.

From the standpoint of selling medicine, though, medicine

shows could still go. Medicine and ailments are the easiest con of all—these days that's where people are most vulnerable, on the subject of their health. Look at all those people trailing off to Sweden to some woman to be healed. Or going to the Philippines to be operated on by those so-called psychic doctors. Pretending to pull out fake tumors with their bare hands without making an incision—shoot!

(In March 1975, a Federal Trade Commission judge ruled that psychic surgery was "pure and unmitigated fakery.")

Arthritis, now, that's one there's a million "cures" for, because we still don't know exactly how to treat it. There must be thousands of people around the country wearing copper bracelets to cure arthritis. Another arthritis "cure" that some folks try is a pair of heel plates they put inside their shoes, one copper, one zinc.

We keep hoping maybe we've hit on an arthritis cure, even though we don't understand how it works. Out in my little town the latest craze for curing arthritis is gun oil, penetrating oil. Everybody is spraying and rubbing gun oil on their joints. A lady who hadn't walked for years can take herself to the bathroom now. People don't know why, but it works. Maybe there's some property in the oil that helps. Or maybe it's just because people believe in it.

Yes, it's a shame we don't have medicine shows today, with all the gimmicks and products we could come up with. If I had a medicine show now, I'd sell health foods, because nobody wants to get old with the rest of us. I'd find something that worked a little bit, and I'd have an elaborate setup for the pitch, how this health food would add twenty years to people's lives and smooth out all their wrinkles. Maybe I'd sell a food made from apricots from that part of south Russia where some people live to be one hundred and twenty years old or more. Sure, the customers would buy it. Why, they're all dreaming about the fountain of youth—they're already sold.

Conning—oh yes! No problem with the con, if you tried to revive the medicine show. It's easier than ever to con people today. You see, nowadays people think they're smart, they've learned a lot, they know it all. So you just let a feller go, he'll con himself. Look at all the big-time cons he bites on—real estate frauds, home improvement frauds, credit card frauds.

Because people now are brainwashed from the time they are born. They're used to being persuaded by propaganda from the press, television, radio. Result, if you can convince people they'll be thinner, healthier, richer, or live longer, they'll buy it. They're hungry for this kind of stuff. If you told people they'd be healthier by eating a certain kind of dirt, they'd eat it.

You talk about pitch doctors being con artists, television makes them look like pikers. How? The TV sell is hard sell—they say just enough about a product to make it look good but not enough to perjure themselves. Every show on television is geared to sell something, not only products but ideas, too. Like anti-gun laws, black-and-white racial ideas. They tell the Indians' story, or they're leaning against politicians. I guess that part is all right, and yet I still think television is the worst thing that happened in the world. Because it's made people too smart—*surface smart.* Now everybody's an expert. He thinks.

I'd like to go back to the medicine show days, roll it back to, say, 1937. We lived slower then. People those days had time to visit each other, to walk barefoot down the street, to run to see a tramp medicine show. We've gotten off the track. People need to be a little dumb, not so worldly. It was better when a feller was a little more trusting and didn't think he knew everything. Because he don't anyway.

If we could go back to those medicine show days, I'd razzle-dazzle a feller, and he'd go away happy.

BIBLIOGRAPHY

BOOKS

Besant, Walter, *The World Went Very Well Then.* New York: Harper & Bros., 1888

Bowman, Bredvold, Greenfield, Weirick, eds., *Essays for College English.* Boston: D. C. Heath and Company, 1915. Articles: Thomas Nixon Carver, "Problems of Rural Social Life"; Frederick J. Turner, "The Significance of the Frontier in American History"; Woodrow Wilson, "The Social Center: A Means of Common Understanding"

Carson, Gerald, *One for a Man, Two for a Horse.* Garden City, N.Y.: Doubleday & Company, Inc., 1961

Carter, Kate B., *Heart Throbs of the West.* Salt Lake City: Daughters of Utah Pioneers, 1939

Douglas, William A., *A History of Dentistry in Colorado, 1859–1959.* Denver: Colorado State Dental Association. Boulder, Colo.: Johnson Publishing Co., 1959

Encyclopædia Britannica, 1961: "Quackery"

Furnas, J. C., *The Americans: A Social History of the United States, 1587–1914.* New York: G. P. Putnam's Sons, 1969

Gilbert, Douglas, *American Vaudeville: Its Life and Times.* New York: Dover Publications, 1940

Hechtlinger, Adelaide, *The Great Patent Medicine Era.* New York: Grosset & Dunlap, Inc., 1970

Holbrook, Stewart, *The Golden Age of Quackery.* New York: The Macmillan Company, 1959

McNeal, Violet, *Four White Horses and a Brass Band.* Garden City, N.Y.: Doubleday & Company, Inc., 1947

Pickard, Madge E., and Buley, R. Carlyle, *The Midwest Pioneer: His Ills, Cures and Doctors.* Crawfordsville, Ind.: R. E. Banta, 1945

Webber, Malcolm, *Medicine Show.* Caldwell, Idaho: Caxton Printers, Ltd., 1941

The World Book Encyclopedia, 1965: "Drug Regulation"

Young, James Harvey, *The Medical Messiahs.* Princeton, N.J.: Princeton University Press, 1967

PERIODICALS

Barnes, Sisley, "Medicine Shows: Duped, Delighted." *Smithsonian*, Jan. 1975

Burt, William P., "Back Stage with a Medicine Show Fifty Years Ago." *Colorado Magazine*, July 1942

Clifford, F. J., "The Medicine Show," *Frontier Times*, Nov. 1930

Edstrom, David, "Medicine Man of the '80s." *Reader's Digest*, June 1938

Fox, William Price, "The Late Great Medicine Show." *Travel and Leisure*, Dec. 1974

Frontier Times, "A Bunco of the '80s: The Diamond King." Apr.–May 1953

Gibson, Arrell M., "Medicine Show." *American West*, Feb. 1967

Haugaard, Kay, "Medicine Show." *True West*, Jan.–Feb. 1964

McNamara, Brooks, "The Indian Medicine Show." *Educational Theatre Journal*, Dec. 1971

———, "Medicine Shows: American Vaudeville in the Marketplace." *Theatre Quarterly* (U.K.), May–July 1974

The Medical Investigator, July 1897

Missouri Historical Review, "Picturesque Medicine Shows Combined Entertainment with Salesmanship," July 1951

Mundell, Charles S., "Some Personal Experiences in Medicine Show Buncombe." *Haldeman-Julius Monthly*, 1925

Nathan, George Jean, "The Medicine Men." *Harper's Weekly*, Sept. 9, 1911

Noell, Mae, "Some Memories of a Medicine Show Performer." *Theatre Quarterly* (U.K.), May–July 1974

Robbins, Peggy, "A Brief History of Quack Medicines in America." *The American Legion Magazine*, March 1975

Sappington, Joe, "The Passing of the Medicine Show." *Frontier Times*, Jan. 1930

Stout, Wesley, "Med Show," as told by Dr. N. T. Oliver (Nevada Ned). *The Saturday Evening Post*, Sept. 14, 1929

———, "Alagazam: The Story of Pitchmen, High and Low," as told by Nevada Ned Oliver. *The Saturday Evening Post*, Oct. 19, 1929

Tully, Jim, "The Giver of Life." *American Mercury*, June 1928

NEWSPAPERS

Central City Register-Call, "Doctor Haskell," July 10, 1872

Daily Gate City, "It Happened in Keokuk," Nov. 1874–Apr. 1875

The Denver Post, "Psychic Surgery Ruled 'Phony' by F.T.C. Judge," March 15, 1975

Downing, Robert, "Bygone Medicine Shows Touted Benefits—Mostly the Huckster's." *The Denver Post, Roundup Magazine,* Jan. 1975

INTERVIEWS

Cliff and Allene Mann, Rangely, Colo., 1975

OTHER INFORMATION

Federal Trade Commission, Kansas City, Mo., and Washington, D.C.

GLOSSARY

Almshouse
a home for the poor, provided by private financing

At liberty
unemployed

Ballyhoo
n. a flamboyant means of attracting attention to a product to be sold or a show to be presented; v. to talk extravagantly or to provide introductory entertainment, leading to a product or the main show

Bitters
a liquid tonic composed of bitter plant products and, usually, alcohol

Bones
small clappers that are rattled together rhythmically; originally small animal bones were used; later, wooden sticks or spoons

Buck-and-wing dance
a solo tap dance with sharp foot accents, springs into the air, leg flings and heel clicks

Carnie
a carnival worker

Clog dance
    a dance in which performer wears thick-soled shoes and beats out a clattering rhythm

Double
    to perform two or more roles

Double paddle
    two pieces of board hinged to make loud smack when swung by handle

Electuary
    a confection; medicine coated with candy or mixed with honey or sweet syrup

Emetic
    an agent that induces vomiting

End men
    the men at each end of the line of performers in a minstrel show who engage in comic dialogue with the interlocutor

Fright wig
    a comic wig of hair that bushes out, sometimes carrot-colored; can be wired to make hairs stand out or rise up when string is pulled

Gig
    (from a pronged spear for catching fish) v. to stick a customer for money; n. a medicine showman's plan of action for obtaining money from a customer

Handbill
    a small printed advertising sheet to be distributed by hand

Hoecakes
    (from their being baked on the blade of a hoe, originally) small cakes made of cornmeal or flour, fried like hotcakes

Hoofer
    a professional dancer

Interlocutor
    a man in the middle of the line in a minstrel show who questions the end men to produce comic repartee

Jamb worker
>(from gambit) one who sells worthless products or services; usually an itinerant who travels on before the customer discovers he's been cheated

Jew's harp
>a small lyre-shaped instrument with a metal tongue; played by placing between teeth and striking the metal tongue with the finger to achieve twanging tones

Jug band
>a collection of persons playing earthen jugs of varying sizes; resonant sounds are produced by blowing into the opening of the jug while humming the melody

Lancet
>a sharp-pointed and usually two-edged surgical knife used to make small incisions

Leech
>carnivorous or bloodsucking worm, usually freshwater; used to bleed patients; because of that common practice, long ago physicians also were nicknamed "leeches"

Limewater
>water containing calcium carbonate or calcium sulfate in solution; if combined with carbon dioxide, as when a person exhales into it, it becomes cloudy; any acid, such as vinegar, clears the clouded water

Nostrum
>a medicine of secret formula, recommended by its preparer but usually lacking general repute; a questionable medicine

Piker
>a gambler for small sums

Pitch
>a high-pressure sales talk; hence pitch doctor, a high-pressure medicine salesman

Placebo
>a medication of inert or innocuous ingredients, given to please or soothe the patient

Poultice
>a soft medicated mass, often heated, spread on cloth and applied to the skin, usually for sores

Proprietary medicine
>medicine whose name and formula belong to the maker; patent medicine, commonly so called whether the name was registered with the U.S. Patent Office or not

Purgative
>a medication that causes evacuation of the bowels; colloquially called a physic; a laxative is generally a milder form of a purgative

Quack doctor
>a pretender to medical skill or knowledge

Road stake
>money for traveling and for living purposes while on the road

Rube
>an unsophisticated person living in a rural area

Sarsaparilla
>a tonic or beverage made from the dried roots of the vine smilax

Shill
>one who acts as a decoy for a pitchman or gambler, making purchases or bets to encourage others to do the same

Skid row
>a district of cheap saloons and flophouses frequented by vagrants, alcoholics and migrant workers

Soft-shoe dance
>a rhythmic dance done in soft-soled shoes without metal taps

Spiel
>a fluent, extravagant talk; *see* Pitch

Sticks (the)
>rural areas far removed from cities

Straight man
>an entertainer who feeds lines to a comedian; sometimes the master of ceremonies

Tinker
>a traveling peddler of pots, pans and notions, who might also mend stoves and lawn mowers and sharpen scissors, knives and saws

Tow sack
>large sack made of loosely woven burlap; gunnysack

Tramp show
>a small, unpretentious show traveling from town to town without much advance announcement

Vaudeville
>a light stage entertainment combining a variety of unrelated acts that might include comedy skits, dancing, songs, acrobatics or performing animals

Vermifuge
>a concoction designed to expel worms from the body

Index

Numbers in *italics* refer to illustrations.

Adams, Samuel Hopkins, 71–74, *73*, 80–82, 85, 115
Advertisements, 19, 25, 26, *27*, *31*, 32, 42, *52*, 67, *68*, 70, 71, *83*, 85, 95, 115
  mail-order sales, 3, 70, 71, 82
  See also Publicity and promotion
Alcohol in medicines, 8, 20, 42, 67, 70, 74, 79–80, *81*, 82, *86*, 114
American Medical Association, Bureau of Investigation, 85
Ayer's Sarsaparilla, 67

Ballard, W.A., 70–71
Ballyhoo, 2, 8–9, 40, 42, 43, 47, 54–57, *59*, 90, 101
  See also Publicity and promotion
Balrod, Professor, 47
Barnum, P.T., *83*
Bartok, Doc, 45
Berry, Dr. J.L., 37
Besant, Walter, *The World Went Very Well Then*, 22

Big Sensation Medicine Company, 39, 40, 77
Bigelow, Charles ("Texas Charlie"), 28–32, *30*, *31*, 34, 105, 109, 113
Birney's Catarrh Powder, 80–81
Bitters, *38*, 67, 79, 80
Black Diamond Snake Oil, 20
Black, Ray, 43, 47–48
Black-Draught, 8, 83–84
Bristol's Sarsaparilla, 80
Brother Jonathan, 43, 50–51, 74, 104, 108
Buley, R. Carlyle. *See* Pickard, Madge E.
Burt, William P., 39, 40, *96*, 112

Castoria, 83
Catarrh remedies, 66, 67, 77–79, *78*, 80–81, 82
Chattanooga Medicine Company, 84
Chinese Herb Remedies, 37
Chippewa Indian Medicine Company, 34

131

Clifford, F.J., 94, 100
Clough, Jack, 97
Collier's Weekly, 71, 73, 85
Cough remedies, 36, 67–70, 80, 110
Cramp, Arthur J., 85–87

Dances, 10, 12, 23, 36, 41, 95, 97
Dentistry, 40, 49, 75, 77
Depression, the, 3, 4, 7, 16, 18, 21
Diamond King, 43, 48–50, 77, 104
Doan's Kidney Pills, 67
Doc McDonald's Indian Medicine Show, 4–12, *17*, 20, 22, 88, 100
  Doc McDonald's Magic Corn Salve, 7, 8, 9, 12, 20
  McDonald's Compound, 8, 11, 12, 20, 61, 83
Doctor Heady's Peerless Remedy, 57
Dr. Bull's Cough Syrup, 80
Dr. Hartman's Peruna. *See* Peruna
Dr. Herrick's Almanac, 67
Dr. Sage's remedy, 78
Du Bois, Madame, 54

Edwards, Col. T.A., 66
Electric Belts, 37, 70, 106
Elixir of Life, 26
Entertainment, 3, 7, 10, 12, 21, 22, 23, 26, 40, 42, 43, 88–103, 117–18
  comedy routines, 3, 9, 10, 26, 41, 89, 92–94
  contests, 11, 100
  magicians, 19, 26, 39–40
  plays, 10–11, 26, 27
  show set-ups, 9–10, 33, 34, 35, 40, 45, 47, 117
  strong-man acts, 41, 95, 97–98
  Wild West shows, 34

Federal Drug Administration (FDA), 115, *116*
Federal Trade Commission (FTC), 115, 120

Ferdon, Jim, 36–39, *38*, 105, 106, 113
Field, Eugene, 99
Flagg, E.H., 29
Furnas, J.C., *The Americans,* 65–67

Give Back operators, 110–11
Giver of Life, 50–51, 74, 108
  See also Brother Jonathan
Government regulations on medicine, 20, 25, 41, 71, 73, 74, 75, 115, *116*
  Federal Drug Administration, 115, *116*
  Federal Trade Commission, 115, 120
  lack of regulation, 3, 20, 25
  licenses, 101, 109, 111
  Narcotics Act of 1914, 74
  Pure Food and Drug Act of 1907, 73, 74, 109
Great Pizzaro. *See* Ferdon, Jim

Hadacol, 42, 85, 98
Haldeman-Julius Monthly, 56–57
Hamlin's Wizard Oil Company, 2, 34–36, 39, 74, 82, 99, 110
  Hamlin's Blood and Liver Pills, 36
  Hamlin's Cough Balsam, 36
  Hamlin's Wizard Oil, 36, 58
Hammer, Arthur, 101
Hashalew, Old Doc. *See* Popple, Professor
Haskell, Dr., 40
Heady, James ("Doc"), 56–57
Healy, John E., 28–29, 32, 34, 76, 105, 109
  Healy's Hibernian Minstrels, 29
  Healy's Liver Pad Concert Company, 76
Health care in America
  medical training, 24–25, 51, 63–64
  natural cures and folk medicine, 7, 24, 28, 51–53, 60, 64, 79, 83–84, 105, 115, 120

19th century, 24–25, 51–53, 63–67, 83
20th century, 114–15, 120
See also Government regulations on medicine
Herbs of Joy, 34, 42
Herbs of Life, 29
High German Doctor, 22–23, 58
Holbrook, Stewart, *The Golden Age of Quackery*, 85
Hood's Sarsaparilla, 67, 68
Hostetter's Celebrated Stomach Bitters, 80

Indian Doctor's Receipt Book, The, 28
Indian Elixir, 60
Indian Guide to Health, The, 28
Indian Root, 47
Indians in medicine shows, 4–7, 18, 19, 20, 22, 26–34, 36, 58, 59, 66, 85, 113
    companies: *See* Chippewa Indian Medicine Company; Doc McDonald's Indian Medicine Show; Kickapoo Indian Medicine Company; Oregon Indian Medicine Company
    Tribes: Cherokee, 7, 19, 33; Choctaw, 7; Cree, 33; Iroquois, 32–33; Modoc, 66; Nez Percé, 66, 67; Pawnee, 33; Sioux, 33

Jumbo, the elephant, 83

Ka-Ton-Ka tonic, 66, 67
Kickapoo Indian Medicine Company, 2, 28–34, 37, 57, 67, 69, 74, 76, 82, 85, 105, 109–10
    Kickapoo Indian Oil, 29, 67–70, 85
    Kickapoo Indian Prairie Plant, 67
    Kickapoo Indian Sagwa, 28, *30*, 32–34, 58, 67, 85, 110
    Kickapoo Indian Salve, 67, 69

King of Forceps, 40, 77
King of Pain liniment, 29
King of the Medicine Men. *See* Lighthall, Jim

Laxatives (physics, purgatives), 8, 21, 63, 65, 67, 79, *83*, 83–84, 110
Leavitt's Monster Minstrels, *91*
LeBlanc, Dudley J. (State Senator), 42, 98
Leeches, 65
    bleeding, 65–67
Lighthall, Jim ("Doc"), 34, 36–37, 100, 105
Liniments. *See* Ointments and liniments
Liver pads, 29, 76–77

McCrillus' Standard Remedies, 99–100
McDonald, Jude ("Doc"), 4–9, 11, 12, 13, 15, 18, 20, 28, 43, 60–61, 77, 100, 106, 113, 117
McNeal, Violet, 43, 53, 54–56, 61, 74–75, 77, 79, 104–5, 108, 109, 111, 113
    Four White Horses and a Brass Band, 54, 61
    Tiger Fat, 54–55, 74–76
    Vital Sparks, 55, 74–75, 100
McNeal, Will, 54, 105
Maloney, Jonathan. *See* Brother Jonathan
Mann, Alice, 4, 5, 13, 16, 19
Mann, Allene, 88, 119
Mann, Cliff, 4–10, 6, 12–21, 22, 28, 42, 43, 60–61, 63, 77, 82, 85, 88, 94, 98, 105–6, 113, 117–21
Mann, Eugene Richard ("Happy"), 4–10, 12, 14, 15, 16–18, *17*, 43, 90, 105–6, 117–19
Mann, Jodi, 119
Mann, Joe, 5, *8*

133

Mason, H.D., *Symptoms and Treatment of All Disease*, 64–65
Medical Investigator, The, 70–71, 72, 80–81
Minard's Liniment, 67
Minstrel shows, 23, 29, 90–92
Mundell, Charles S., 56–57, 106, 108
Music and musicians, 2, 3, 4, 10, 12, 17, 23, 26, 29, 36, 37, 40, 41, 42, 58, 89, 90, 92, 94–95, 97

Narcotic drugs, 49, 74, 77, 80–82, 105, 114
National Pitchmen's and Salesmen's Protective Association, 112
Nevada Ned. *See* Oliver, Nevada Ned
Nez Percé Catarrh Snuff, 66, 67
Noell, Mae, 94
North American Indian Doctor, The, 28

Ointments and liniments, 2, 3, 7, 8, 9, 12, 16, 20, 29, 34, 54–55, 66, 67, 69, 70, 74–76, 83, 90, 96, 99, 104, 109, 112–13, 114, 119
Oliver, Nevada Ned, 28–29, 32, 33–34, 37, 45, 82, 110–11, 113
Oregon Indian Medicine Company, 66, 67
  Ka-Ton-Ka tonic, 66, 67
  Nez Percé Catarrh Snuff, 66, 67
  War Paint Ointment, 66
Oriental Ointment, 99–100

Paine's Celery Compound, 81
Pasteur, Madame V., *See* McNeal, Violet
Patent (proprietary) medicines, 3, 25, 28, 40, 41, 67, 70, 74, 83, 85, 104
  ingredients, 1, 8, 37, 42, 48, 51, 67, 74–75, 82, 83, 84, 120
  See also Alcohol in medicines; Narcotic drugs
Patten, Z.C., 84

Peruna, 80, 85, *86*
Pickard, Madge E., and Buley, R. Carlyle, *The Midwest Pioneer: His Ills, Cures and Doctors,* 51
Pigeon Drop con, 44
Pinkham, Lydia E., 71
  Lydia E. Pinkham's Vegetable Compound for Female Complaints, 67, 71, 79
Popple, Professor, 26, 28
Poultices, 65–67
Prince Nanzetta, 43, 53
Princess Iola, 54
Princess Lotus Blossom. *See* McNeal, Violet
Profits, 3, 9, 34, 37–39, 42, 49, 50–51, 55, 57, 70, 104–5, 110
Publicity and promotion, 2–3, 8–9, 26, 40–41, 47–48, 90, 118–19
  See also Advertisements; Ballyhoo
Punja, Doctor, 60
Pure Food and Drug Act, 73, 74, 109

Quaker Medicine Company, 36–39, *38,* 58, 105
Queen of Forceps, 77
Queen of Medicine Shows. *See* McNeal, Violet

Riley, James Whitcomb, 99–100
Roosevelt, Theodore, 74

Sagwa. *See* Kickapoo Indian Medicine Company, Kickapoo Indian Sagwa
Sarsaparillas. *See* Tonics and sarsaparillas
Saturday Evening Post, The, 34, 45
Shaker Medicine Company, 39
Shell game, 12
Silk Hat Harry, 43, 61–62
Simmons, A.O., 84
Sloat, Dr., 40
Smart's Rheumatic and Neuralgic Paste, 67

Smith, Peter, *Indian Doctor's Dispensatory, The,* 28
Spanish Oil, 49, 77
Spanish Trunk Swindle, 44
Standard Remedies. *See* McCrillus' Standard Remedies
Stowe, Harriet Beecher. *See Uncle Tom's Cabin*

Tapeworm remedies, 34, 67, 76
Temperance Movement, 60, 79–80
Testimonials, 3, 80, *81,* 85–87, *86*
Texas Charlie. *See* Bigelow, Charles
Thedford, J.H., 84
Thunder Cloud, Chief, 32
Thurber, Curly, 108
Tiger Fat, 54–55, 74–76
Tonics and sarsaparillas, 2, 3, 7, 8, 11, 12, 16, 20, 28, 46, 47, 61, 66, 67, *68,* 70, 74, 79, 80, 83, *86,* 104

Ton-Ko-Ko Medicine Show, 40, 58, 95–97, 100
Townsend, C.M., 99
   Townsend's Cholera Balm, 99
Transportation and travel, 1, 7, 13–15, 20, 34–36, 40

Uncle Tom's Cabin, 26, 27

Vaudeville. *See* Entertainment
Vigor of Life, 39, 42
Vin Vita, 70
Vital Sparks, 5, 74–75, 100

Wagner, Happy Cal, 89
Wallace, Big Foot Bill, 106
Webber, Malcolm, *Medicine Show,* 95–98
Wellington, J.W., 40

Yellowstone, Doctor, 29
Your Uncle Dutchey, 39–40, 89

PICTURE CREDITS

Grateful acknowledgement is made for use of illustrations:

The Bettmann Archive, 46
Brown Brothers, 27, 59, 91, 107
Denver Public Library, Western History Department, 2, 41
The Historical Society of Colorado Library, 96
Mann, Cliff, 6, 17
The New-York Historical Society, 30 and back of jacket, 35 and front of jacket, 52, 68, 69, 78, 81, 83, front of jacket
The New York Library, Picture Collections, 38, 73, 76
The New York Public Library at Lincoln Center, The Theatre Collection of the Performing Arts, Astor, Lenox and Tilden Foundations, 31, 67